COLOURS AROUND ME
Yellow

Anita Loughrey

QED Publishing

What is yellow?

Yellow is a colour.

This is the colour yellow.

Look at the picture of the playroom.

What can you see in the playroom that is yellow?

Answer: The dump truck is yellow.

Finding yellow

Point to the things
that are yellow.

How many yellow
things can you see?

Matching yellow

Look at the flowers.

Point to the two yellow flowers.

Monkey trouble

Help the monkey through the maze to get to the banana tree.

How many yellow bananas does the monkey pass on the way?

Answer: 5 yellow bananas

Yellow shapes

Yellow things can be different shapes.

How many
yellow squares
can you see?

How many
yellow circles
can you see?

Answer: 2 yellow squares, 3 yellow circles

How many yellow
rectangles can you see?

How
many yellow
triangles can
you see?

What yellow shapes
can you see around you?

Big and small

Yellow things can be different sizes.

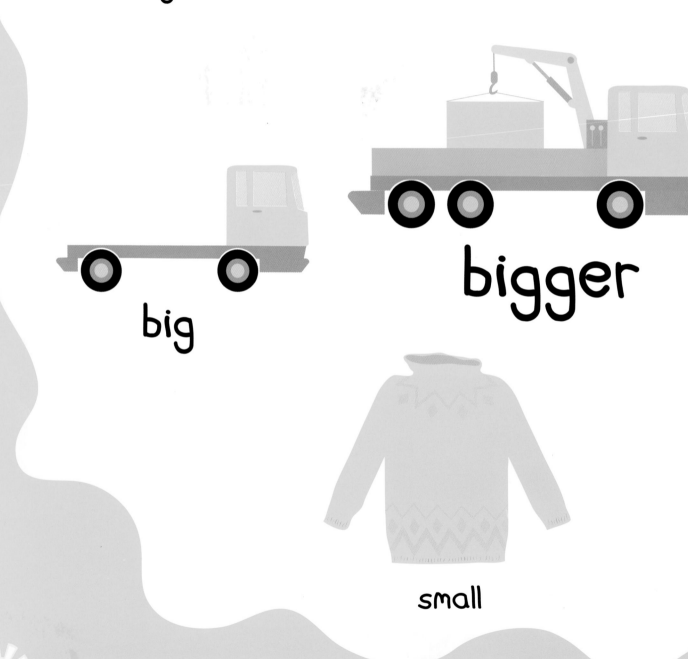

big

bigger

small

biggest

smaller

smallest

Odd ones out

Some things here
are the wrong colour.

balloon

lemon

ladybird

apple

leaf

12

sun

cabbage

butterfly

chick

Which things should be yellow?

Answer: The lemon, the sun and the chick should be yellow.

Shades of yellow

Yellow can be different shades.

yellow

dark yellow

dark yellow

light yellow

yellow and
light yellow

light yellow

What shades of yellow
can you see around you?

Yellow at the palace

Can you find these yellow things at the palace?

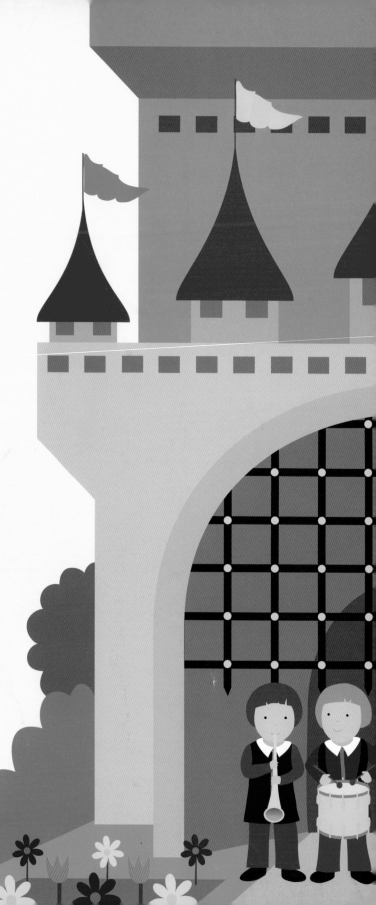

crown

trumpet

drum

flower

flag

dress

cup

Have you ever
seen any of these
yellow things?

17

Yellow at the safari park

Point to all the yellow things you can see at the safari park.

jeep

banana

hat

snake

lion

giraffe

cheetah

Have you ever been to a
safari park? Did you see
these animals there?

Yellow is for sunshine

Point to all the yellow things you can see at the sunny beach.

bucket and spade

sandcastle

parasol

towel

sun

sunhat

sunglasses

What other
yellow things
might you see
at the beach?

Yellow is for happiness

The children are happy playing in the park. Point to the yellow things they are playing with.

 ball

 bicycle

 car

swing

slide

see-saw

climbing frame

which of these yellow things have you played with?

23

Notes for parents and teachers

This book has been designed to help children to recognize the colour yellow and to distinguish yellow from other colours. The vibrant activities make learning fun and use the environment around them to reinforce what they have learned.

• Read the instructions to the child. Allow time for the child to think about the activity. Encourage them to discuss what they see.

• Praise the child if they recognize the items in the book. If any of the items are unfamiliar, explain what they are and where they might be found.

• If possible, take the child into the environment you have talked about so that they can observe items pictured in this book. Encourage the child to spot yellow objects using ideas from this book.

• Remember to keep it fun. Stop before the child gets tired or loses interest, then continue on another day. Children learn best when they are relaxed and enjoying themselves. It is best to help them experience new concepts in small steps.

Other activities you could try:

• Play games such as 'I spy': saying "I spy with my little eye a yellow thing beginning with...". If the child is not yet familiar with the alphabet, you could say the initial sound of the word rather than the letter name.

• Cut pictures from catalogues and magazines of different-coloured objects and ask the child to sort them, or match them to the pictures in this book.

• Ask the child what yellow things they can see when you are outside, at home, or looking in other books.

• Experiment with colour using different media such as paint, crayons, pastels and coloured paper.

Illustrator: Sue Hendra
Editor: Lauren Taylor
Designer: Fiona Hajée
Educational consultant: Jillian Harker

Copyright © QED Publishing 2011

First published in the UK in 2011 by
QED Publishing
A Quarto Group company
226 City Road
London EC1V 2TT

www.qed-publishing.co.uk

A catalogue record for this book is available from the British Library.

ISBN 978 1 84835 536 1

Printed in China

When? Where? How?

This book takes you on a journey through 10,000 years of history, starting with the very first farmers and ending with the collapse of the Roman Empire.

Roman soldier

When did it happen?

Most of the events in this book happened before the birth of Christ. These dates are shown by the letters "BC" (before Christ). For example, 50BC means 50 years before the birth of Christ. BC dates are counted back from 1BC, so 100BC is earlier than 50BC. There is a timeline across the bottom of each double page to help you see when events took place.

The letters "AD" show that an event happened after Christ's birth. AD stands for *anno Domini*, which is Latin for "in the year of the Lord".

If a date has a letter "c." in front of it, this means that experts are not sure exactly when the event happened. The "c." stands for *circa*, which means "about" in Latin.

Where did it happen?

There are maps throughout the book to show you exactly where things happened. You can also check which area of the world you are reading about by looking at the bottom corner of each page. The areas of the world are shown on the map below.

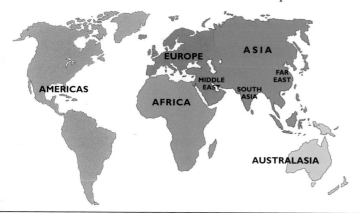

AMERICAS · EUROPE · ASIA · MIDDLE EAST · FAR EAST · SOUTH ASIA · AFRICA · AUSTRALASIA

How do we know?

The only way to find out about people in the ancient world is to look at the things they left behind. Experts who dig up and study these objects are called archaeologists. New discoveries are being made all the time, so our knowledge of the ancient world is always changing.

Archaeologists at work

In ancient times, people's possessions were often buried with them. Objects, such as weapons, tools, pots, furniture and fragments of cloth, tell us a lot about how people lived.

Celtic neckband

Tombs and buildings often contain statues, wall paintings and mosaics showing scenes from daily life.

Sumerian mosaic showing soldiers in battle

Ancient writing has been found on pieces of clay, on the walls of buildings and on scrolls of papyrus (a type of paper). These writings tell us about ancient rulers, laws and religious beliefs.

The First Farmers

The very first people hunted wild animals, caught fish and gathered nuts, plants and berries to eat. It was thousands of years before people learned how to farm.

Farming began in the Middle East, in an area we call the Fertile Crescent. Around 10,000BC, the weather there became wetter and warmer, so plants could grow more easily.

Cutting wheat with a tool called a sickle

People noticed that seeds which had fallen on the ground grew into plants. They began to collect the seeds and plant them on purpose. The first crops grown like this were wild wheat and barley.

Around the same time, people learned how to tame animals. This meant that they always had plenty of meat, milk and wool. They could also use cattle for working in the fields.

These pots were made by early farmers.

Once people knew how to farm, they no longer needed to move around to hunt for food. They began to settle down in villages and had time to learn new skills, such as spinning, weaving and making pots.

In this picture of an early village, one house has been cut away to let you see inside.

Çatal Hüyük

MEDITERRANEAN SEA

Euphrates

Tigris

Jericho

Nile

RED SEA

Map of the Fertile Crescent

Fertile Crescent

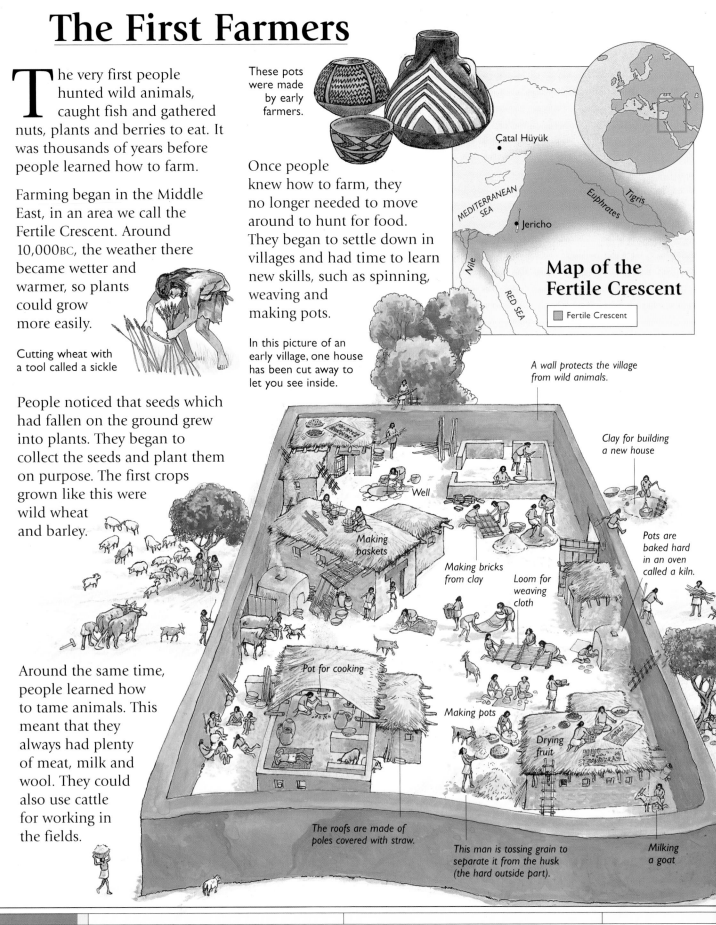

A wall protects the village from wild animals.

Clay for building a new house

Pots are baked hard in an oven called a kiln.

Well

Making baskets

Making bricks from clay

Loom for weaving cloth

Pot for cooking

Making pots

Drying fruit

The roofs are made of poles covered with straw.

This man is tossing grain to separate it from the husk (the hard outside part).

Milking a goat

THE MIDDLE EAST

10,000BC   5000BC   4000BC   3000BC

The First Towns

Slowly, small farming villages grew into towns. The oldest town that has been found so far is at Jericho.

Jericho

The people of Jericho lived in small, round houses made of mud bricks.

A cutaway picture of a house in Jericho

Dead people were buried underneath the houses. Their skulls may have been put on display, as a way of showing respect.

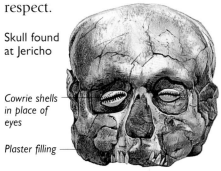

Skull found at Jericho

Cowrie shells in place of eyes

Plaster filling

Jericho grew rich by trading with other communities, and people in the nearby villages became jealous. To protect themselves, the people of Jericho built a massive stone wall around the town.

Building the walls of Jericho

Çatal Hüyük

Çatal Hüyük (pronounced chatal hoo-yook) was the largest of the early towns. Around 6,000 people lived there.

This cutaway picture shows part of Çatal Hüyük.

Cattle and goats are kept for meat and milk.

When someone in Çatal Hüyük died, the body was left outside to rot. The skeleton was buried under a bench in the house or in a shrine room, where the people prayed to their gods.

This picture shows a shrine room at Çatal Hüyük.

Painted statue of a goddess

This priest is wearing a leopard skin.

Model of a bull's head with real horns

These priestesses have brought offerings of food and drink for the goddess.

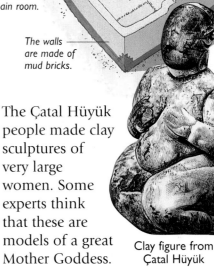

Apple trees

People climb into the houses through a hole in the roof.

If enemies attack, the ladders are pulled up.

All the houses are joined together.

Clay bench covered with reeds

The houses have one main room.

Fireplace

The walls are made of mud bricks.

The Çatal Hüyük people made clay sculptures of very large women. Some experts think that these are models of a great Mother Goddess.

Clay figure from Çatal Hüyük

Important dates

c.10,000BC Farming begins in the Fertile Crescent.

c.8000BC Jericho grows into a wealthy town.

c.6250-5650BC Çatal Hüyük is at its largest.

The First Civilization

The finished bricks are left to dry in the sun.

The flat land of Sumer was good for farming, but there was very little rain. Once a year, the two rivers flooded, soaking the dry ground. The Sumerians built ditches and canals, to store the water and carry it to the fields.

Farmers mending a canal

These people are making mud bricks.

Bricks are shaped in a wooden frame.

Map of Sumer

- Mesopotamia
- City-state

AKKAD

Euphrates

Tigris

SUMER

Uruk ■ ■ Lagash
■ Ur
Eridu ■

PERSIAN GULF

From around 5000BC, farmers settled in the wide valley between the Tigris and Euphrates rivers. This area became known as Mesopotamia, which means "the land between two rivers". The first civilization grew up in Sumer, in the southern part of Mesopotamia.

Farmers were soon able to grow more crops than they could eat. There was no need for everyone to farm, so some people had time to learn specialist skills, such as pottery and weaving.

At first, the Sumerians lived in houses made of reeds. Later, they learned how to make bricks from mud and straw.

Small farming villages gradually grew into huge walled cities, each with its own temple. Each city had a ruler who also had control of the farmland around the city. Cities organized like this are called city-states.

This picture shows part of the Sumerian city of Ur.

This huge, stepped platform is called a ziggurat.

Temple of Nanna, the moon god

A wall protects the city from attacks by other city-states.

The houses are built of mud bricks.

Marketplace

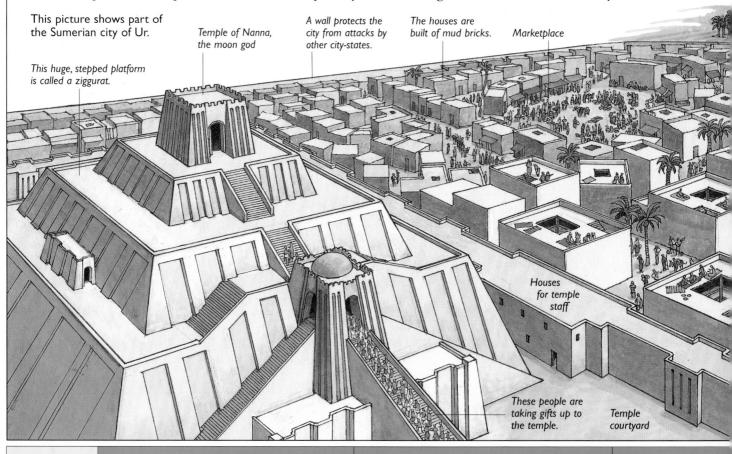

Houses for temple staff

These people are taking gifts up to the temple.

Temple courtyard

The invention of writing

Farmers had to give part of their crop to the temple, and temple officials needed to know if a farmer had paid his share. Writing probably developed as a way of recording this information.

Farmers bringing grain to the temple

1 At first, people drew simple pictures of the objects they wanted to record. These pictures are called pictograms.

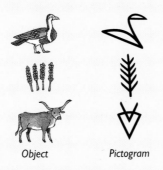

Object   Pictogram

2 The pictures were drawn one below the other on a piece of wet clay.

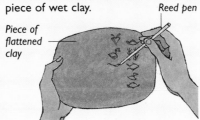

Reed pen

Piece of flattened clay

3 Later, people turned the clay around and wrote from side to side. This stopped them from smudging the pictures they had already drawn.

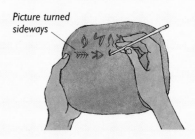

Picture turned sideways

4 Because of the shape of the reed pen, the pictures gradually changed into wedge-shaped symbols, which we call cuneiform writing. Cuneiform means "wedge-shaped".

Cuneiform writing

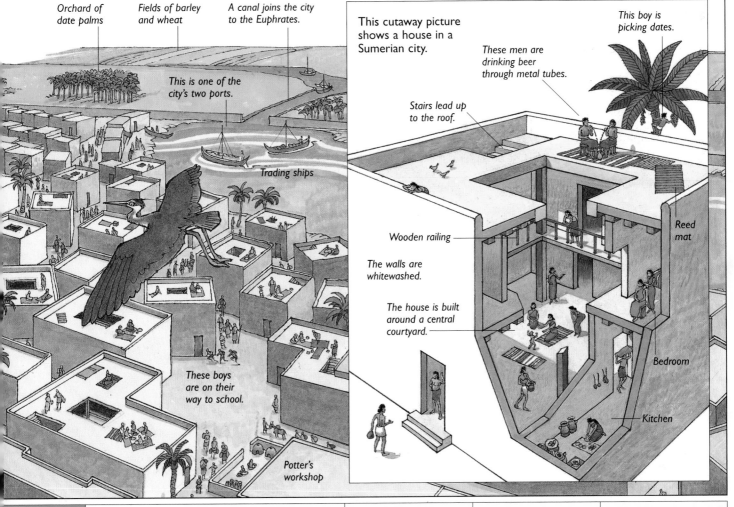

Orchard of date palms

Fields of barley and wheat

A canal joins the city to the Euphrates.

This is one of the city's two ports.

Trading ships

These boys are on their way to school.

Potter's workshop

This cutaway picture shows a house in a Sumerian city.

This boy is picking dates.

These men are drinking beer through metal tubes.

Stairs lead up to the roof.

Wooden railing

The walls are whitewashed.

The house is built around a central courtyard.

Reed mat

Bedroom

Kitchen

THE MIDDLE EAST

Crafts and Trade

There was no stone, metal or strong wood in Sumer, so all these things had to be brought in from other lands. In exchange, the Sumerians sold grain and wool, as well as the pots and metal objects they made in their workshops.

Sumerian traders sailed along canals and rivers into the Persian Gulf and beyond. They traded with merchants from as far away as the Mediterranean Coast in the west and the Indus Valley in the east.

In this picture, merchants are trading at a busy Sumerian market.

This man is selling vegetables.

Wine jars

Basket of grain

Rolls of cloth

Jar of oil

This trader has come from Syria.

These merchants are setting off on a trading expedition.

This man is selling fish.

Metalwork

The Sumerians were skilled metalworkers, and made beautiful objects from gold, silver and copper.

Gold dagger and sheath

Stone is floated down the river on wooden rafts.

Wood from the mountains in the north

This trading ship has just come back from the Persian Gulf.

This trader has brought back a cargo of gold, copper, ivory and semi-precious stones.

A man called a scribe lists the goods as they are unloaded.

Pots and wheels

Sumer had plenty of clay for making pottery. Pots were shaped by hand until around 3500BC, when the potter's wheel was invented.

Pots are baked hard in an oven called a kiln.

Potters at work

Pots are shaped on a wheel.

Boys mix the clay with their feet.

Stone carving

Sculptors carved small stone statues of people praying. People believed that if they placed a statue in the temple, the statue would pray for them.

Stone statue of a temple official

People soon realized that wheels could be attached to carts or chariots, and used for getting around. A donkey pulling a cart could carry three times as much as it could on its back.

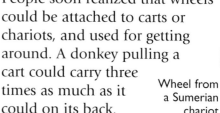

Wheel from a Sumerian chariot

Kings and War

Each city in Sumer was run by a group of noblemen. In times of war, they chose a leader who ruled until the war was over. As wars became more frequent, the war-leaders ruled for longer periods of time. In the end, they became kings who ruled for life, and handed power down to their sons.

Sargon of Akkad

Sargon came from Akkad, the land just north of Sumer. He was a skilled soldier and had control of a huge army. He conquered the whole of Sumer and Akkad, creating the world's first empire.

Sargon of Akkad

This mosaic shows Sumerian soldiers in battle.

Sumerian soldier wearing a cloak and helmet

This is one of the enemy prisoners. He will be killed or sold as a slave.

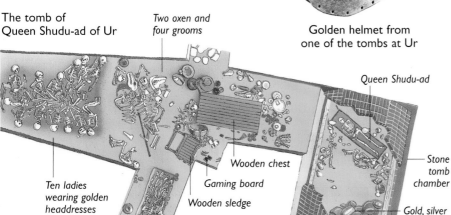

Chariot

Donkeys

This soldier is about to throw his spear.

This is the charioteer. He drives the chariot.

Body of an enemy soldier

The Akkadian Empire lasted nearly 200 years until it was destroyed by a tribe called the Gutians.

Gutian tribesmen

The end of Sumer

The King of Ur won back the Sumerians' land and, for a short time, he ruled all of Sumer and Akkad. Around 2000BC, Sumer was invaded by a tribe known as the Amorites. The land split up into many small states, and later became part of the Babylonian Empire (see page 28).

Royal tombs

The early kings and queens of the city of Ur were buried in large pits filled with amazing treasures. The tombs also contained the bodies of dozens of guards and servants, who had taken poison and died to be with their rulers.

The soldier's long hair fitted in here.

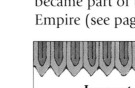

Golden helmet from one of the tombs at Ur

The tomb of Queen Shudu-ad of Ur

Two oxen and four grooms

Queen Shudu-ad

Ten ladies wearing golden headdresses

Wooden chest

Gaming board

Wooden sledge

Five guards

Stone tomb chamber

Gold, silver and copper bowls

Important dates

c.5000BC Farmers settle in Sumer.
c.3500BC The wheel is invented. The first cities are built.
c.3300BC Picture writing is invented.
c.3100BC Cuneiform writing is used.
c.2500BC The royal tombs are built at Ur.
c.2350-2150BC Sumer is part of the Akkadian Empire.
c.2100BC The King of Ur rules Sumer and Akkad. The ziggurat at Ur is built.
c.2000BC The Amorites invade.

THE MIDDLE EAST

| 2000BC | 1000BC | 500BC | AD1 | AD500 |

Farmers of the Nile Valley

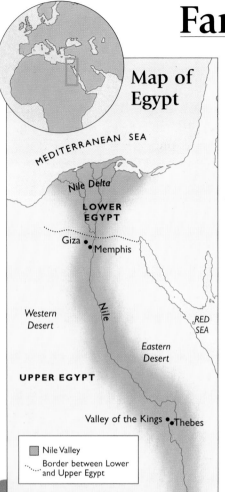

Map of Egypt

MEDITERRANEAN SEA

Nile Delta

LOWER EGYPT

Giza • •Memphis

Western Desert

Nile

RED SEA

Eastern Desert

UPPER EGYPT

Valley of the Kings • •Thebes

☐ Nile Valley
..... Border between Lower and Upper Egypt

Ancient Egypt was a long, narrow country which stretched along the Nile Valley. It was surrounded on both sides by desert.

Villages grew up along the Nile, because the land on either side of the river was good to farm. Every spring, melted snow from the mountains south of Egypt flowed into the Nile, and in July the river flooded. After several months, the water level fell, leaving behind rich, fertile soil.

Gradually, the farming villages of the Nile Valley joined together to form larger communities. By around 3100BC, there were two separate kingdoms, called Lower Egypt and Upper Egypt.

The two kingdoms fought a battle, which was won by King Menes of Upper Egypt. Lower and Upper Egypt became one country, and Menes built a capital city at Memphis for the new, united land.

This carving shows the king of Upper Egypt defeating the ruler of Lower Egypt.

This house has been badly damaged in a flood.

The best fields are nearest the river.

This pole with a bucket is called a shaduf. It lifts water into the fields.

Fishing boats

These men are using sickles to cut the wheat.

Donkeys are used for carrying grain.

Children collect any grain the men have missed.

Ditches and canals store floodwater and carry it to the crops.

AFRICA

10,000BC   5000BC   4000BC   3000BC

10

Crops

The Egyptians grew peas, beans, onions, garlic, leeks, cucumbers, grapes, melons, pomegranates, figs and dates. Grapes and pomegranates were made into wine.

Wine was made by stamping on the grapes, to squeeze out the juice.

The main crops were wheat and barley, which were used to make bread and beer. People sometimes added honey or garlic to their bread to make it more tasty.

Animals

Egyptian farmers kept cattle, sheep, goats, pigs, geese, ducks and pigeons. Cattle were used to work in the fields, as well as for meat. Egypt had very little grassland, so cows were often kept in stalls.

Wooden model of a cow stall

The farmer's year

While the land was flooded, no work could be done in the fields. In November, after the floodwater had gone down, the farmer prepared his fields and planted his crops. In the spring, the whole family helped with the harvest. Then, the farmer mended the ditches that carried water to the fields, ready for the next year's flood.

This tomb painting shows a farmer working in the fields. His wife is scattering seeds on the ground.

This scene shows farmers harvesting their crops.

This monkey has been trained to pick dates.

Cows trample on the grain to separate it from the stalks. This is called threshing.

These women are winnowing - tossing the grain to separate it from the husk (the hard outside part).

Granary for storing grain

Mummies and Pyramids

Experts divide Egyptian history into three main periods of time, called the Old Kingdom, the Middle Kingdom and the New Kingdom. The information on these two pages comes from all three periods.

Coffins

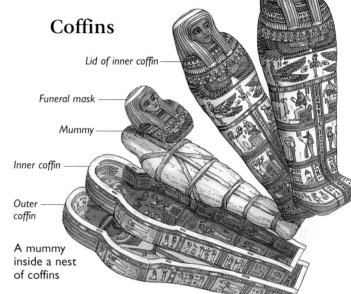

Lid of outer coffin

Lid of inner coffin

Funeral mask

Mummy

Inner coffin

Outer coffin

A mummy inside a nest of coffins

Mummies

The Egyptians tried to stop dead bodies from decaying, because they thought this would allow the dead person to go on living in the Next World. These specially preserved bodies are called mummies.

These pictures show how a mummy was made.

Canopic jar

1 The brain and internal organs were taken out and put in jars called canopic jars.

Natron

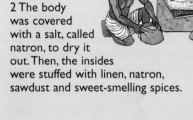

2 The body was covered with a salt, called natron, to dry it out. Then, the insides were stuffed with linen, natron, sawdust and sweet-smelling spices.

3 The body was wrapped in bandages. Lucky charms, called amulets, were placed between the layers.

Anubis mask

4 A mask was put over the mummy's face. A priest dressed as Anubis, god of the dead, prayed over the body.

The first coffins were simple wooden boxes. Later, in the New Kingdom, mummies were put in a nest of two or three human-shaped coffins, one inside the other. These coffins were often brightly painted.

Tomb treasure

The tombs of rich Egyptians were filled with everything the dead person might need in the Next World. Kings were buried with amazing treasures, but robbers soon broke into the tombs and stole the treasure, so very little has been found.

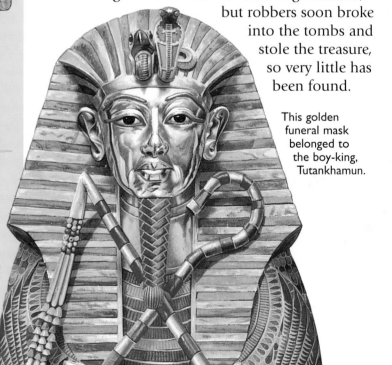

This golden funeral mask belonged to the boy-king, Tutankhamun.

AFRICA

10,000BC	5000BC		4000BC		3000BC

The pyramids

During the Old and Middle Kingdoms, the Egyptians built huge pyramids as tombs for their kings, or pharaohs. There are over 30 pyramids in Egypt, but the most famous ones are at Giza, where three pharaohs and their chief wives are buried.

Khafre will be buried in this pyramid.

This is the mortuary temple. A priest will come here every day to bring food and drink for the spirit of the dead pharaoh.

The smooth sides are meant to look like the rays of the sun.

This is the Great Pyramid. Khafre's father, Khufu, is buried here.

This picture shows the two largest pyramids at Giza, just after the death of the pharaoh Khafre.

These tombs, called mastabas, are for important noblemen.

A huge statue of the Sphinx guards the pyramids. It has a human head and a lion's body.

These small pyramids are for the queen and the pharaoh's other wives.

The Great Pyramid

The Great Pyramid is the largest stone building ever built. It is 147m (482ft) high and contains over two million stone blocks.

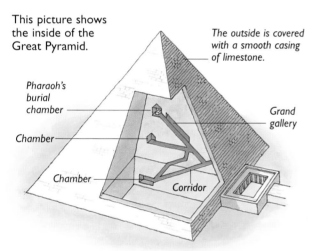

This picture shows the inside of the Great Pyramid.

The outside is covered with a smooth casing of limestone.

Pharaoh's burial chamber

Chamber

Chamber

Grand gallery

Corridor

A passageway links the valley temple to the mortuary temple.

In the valley temple, priests will prepare the pharaoh's body for burial.

A funeral boat brings Khafre's body from his palace at Memphis.

Later tombs

In the New Kingdom, the pharaohs were buried in tombs cut deep into the rock in a hidden valley, called the Valley of the Kings. Although the tombs were hard to find, almost all of them were robbed. The tomb of Tutankhamun was the only one that escaped.

A funeral procession to the Valley of the Kings

Important dates

c.5000BC Farming begins in the Nile Valley.

c.3100BC King Menes unites Upper and Lower Egypt.

c.2686BC The Old Kingdom begins.

c.2180BC The Old Kingdom ends in famine and civil war.

c.2040BC Egypt is reunited. The Middle Kingdom begins.

c.1720BC Egypt is invaded by people called the Hyksos. The Middle Kingdom ends.

AFRICA

2000BC   1000BC   500BC   AD1   AD500

Cities of the Indus Valley

The land in the Indus Valley was good for farming, and the river flooded every year, like the rivers in Sumer and Egypt. Farmers used the floodwater to help them grow more food.

Soon, there was no need for everyone to farm, so some people could do other jobs. People built towns, learned new crafts and started to trade.

By around 2500BC, there were over a hundred towns and cities in the Indus Valley. The two largest were Mohenjo-daro and Harappa.

Map of the Indus Valley

Harappa

Indus

Mohenjo-daro

Lothal

INDIA

ARABIAN SEA

Area where the Indus Valley people lived

The Great Bath

The Great Bath at Mohenjo-daro

Inside the fortress at Mohenjo-daro was a large bathhouse. Priests or rulers may have bathed here before religious ceremonies.

This statue probably shows an Indus Valley priest or ruler.

The city of Mohenjo-daro

Like other Indus Valley cities, Mohenjo-daro was carefully planned. In the middle was a walled fortress, which was built on a huge, man-made hill. Another wall surrounded the city.

This picture shows a typical street in Mohenjo-daro. Part of one house has been cut away to let you see inside.

The houses are built of mud bricks.

In the summer, people sleep on the roof.

The house is built around an open courtyard.

Bedroom

Well

Kitchen

The toilet is connected to a drain that runs under the street.

Oxen are used for pulling carts.

The streets are completely straight.

These men are cleaning the drain.

The Great Granary

Farmers in Mohenjo-daro had to give part of their crop to the city. The grain was stored in a huge granary inside the fortress, so it could be used if there was a bad harvest and food was short.

Grain is stored up here.

Platform for loading grain

A farmer brings his crop of wheat and barley.

The Great Granary at Mohenjo-daro

The walled fortress contains the city's most important buildings.

This woman is buying cotton for a new dress.

This man is selling beads.

Crafts

Potters made cooking pots, storage jars, drinking cups and objects such as children's toys.

Indus Valley pot

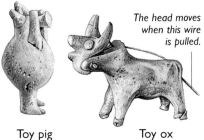

Toy pig

The head moves when this wire is pulled.

Toy ox

Beads for necklaces and bracelets were made from gold, clay and semi-precious stones.

Bead necklace

The farmers of the Indus Valley were the first people to grow cotton and weave it into cloth.

Picking cotton

Stoneworkers made carved seals with writing and pictures of animals on them. Traders may have had their own personal seal, which they used to stamp their name onto pieces of clay.

Carved stone seal of a humped bull

So far, no one has been able to read the Indus Valley writing.

Trade

We know that the Indus people traded with Sumer because their pottery and beads have been found there. They also sold wood, cotton and spices.

A trading ship sets sail from the port at Lothal.

The end of a civilization

From around 1800BC, the Indus Valley civilization began to collapse, but no one is really sure why this happened.

The people may have ruined their farmland by growing too many crops and cutting down too many trees. There may have been quarrels between cities, or a disaster, such as a flood.

Finally, the area was invaded by people known as the Aryans, who brought with them a new way of life (see page 70).

Important dates

c.3500BC Farmers settle in the Indus Valley.

c.2500-1800BC The Indus Valley civilization is at its most successful.

c.1500BC The Aryans invade.

SOUTH ASIA

Europe's First Villages

Red deer

Thousands of years ago, Europe was much colder than it is today, and in the north the land was covered in ice. When the weather warmed up, plants and trees were able to grow again, and wild animals roamed the forests.

Wild boar

People relied on hunting animals and collecting wild plants to eat. They set up camps where they could find food, and moved on when the seasons changed and the food ran out.

Early Europeans

In some places, there was so much food all year that people could settle down. At Lepenski Vir, people built a village on the banks of the Danube, where there was always plenty of fish to catch.

Sculpture of a fish's head from Lepenski Vir

Map of Europe

Skara Brae

Sweet Track

ATLANTIC OCEAN

Danube

Lepenski Vir

MEDITERRANEAN SEA

MALTA

Farmers of the forests

Around 6000BC, life in Europe began to change, as farming spread from the Middle East. In the thick forests that covered most of Europe, farmers cut down trees to make space for fields, and used the wood to build houses.

This picture shows an early European farming village. One house has been cut away to let you see inside.

Vegetables are grown here.

This man is thatching a roof with reeds.

Waste is thrown into a pit.

Pigs feed on acorns in the forest.

Making and decorating clay pots

These boys are collecting hazelnuts.

These men are making a willow fence.

People use stone axes to chop wood.

Stone shelters

Inside a house at Skara Brae

The early Europeans built their houses from whatever they could find nearby. At Skara Brae in the Orkney Islands there were hardly any trees, so people built houses of stone. They even had stone furniture.

Home and dry

In marshy areas, people built long wooden walkways so they could move around easily from one village to another. The Sweet Track in southwestern England stretched for 1.8km (just over a mile).

Farmers on the Sweet Track

Temples and tombs

Stone temples at Tarxien

Some early farmers worked together to create buildings from massive blocks of stone. At Tarxien on the island of Malta, people built temples where they sacrificed animals to their great Mother Goddess.

In western Europe, stone tombs were built and covered with huge mounds of earth. Each tomb had several chambers and had room for up to 40 bodies.

Inside a stone tomb

Pasture for cattle

Fields of wheat and barley

People live in longhouses up to 45m (148ft) long.

A pig roasting on a spit

The roof has caught fire.

Sheep pen

Living area

Part of the wall is plastered with mud.

The walls are made of split logs.

The animals live in one end of the house.

Important dates

c.6000-5000BC Fishing people live at Lepenski Vir.
c.6000-4000BC Farming spreads across most of Europe.
c.4500BC People begin building stone tombs.
c.3800BC The Sweet Track is built.
c.3500BC The first temple is built at Tarxien.
c.3100BC Skara Brae is built.

EUROPE

The Monument Builders

Around 3200BC, people in northwestern Europe began building great circles and lines of standing stones. They also stuck wooden poles in the ground to make circles called wood henges, but most of these have rotted away.

Standing stones at Avebury in southern England

All of these massive monuments were used in religious ceremonies. Some experts think that the mysterious stone circles were also used as giant outdoor calendars.

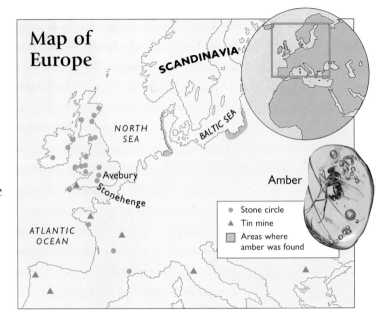

Map of Europe

SCANDINAVIA

NORTH SEA

BALTIC SEA

Avebury

Stonehenge

ATLANTIC OCEAN

Amber

- ● Stone circle
- ▲ Tin mine
- ▢ Areas where amber was found

Building Stonehenge

Stonehenge in southern England is the most spectacular of all the stone circles. It was built in stages over a period of more than a thousand years, and was finally finished around 1500BC.

This picture shows Stonehenge being built.

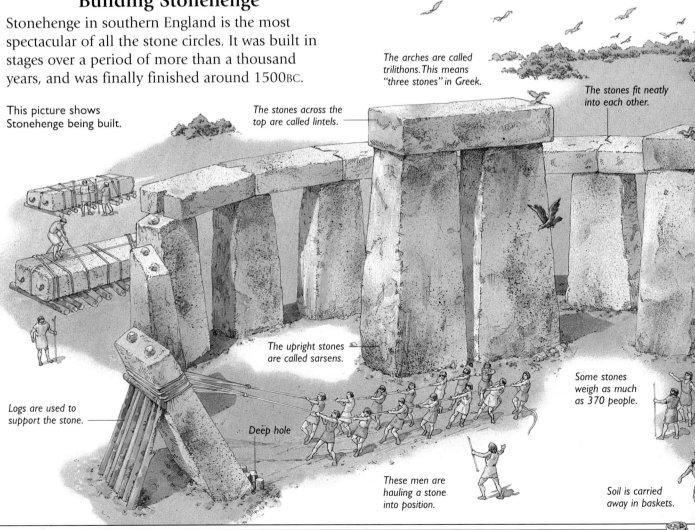

The arches are called trilithons. This means "three stones" in Greek.

The stones across the top are called lintels.

The stones fit neatly into each other.

The upright stones are called sarsens.

Logs are used to support the stone.

Deep hole

These men are hauling a stone into position.

Some stones weigh as much as 370 people.

Soil is carried away in baskets.

EUROPE

10,000BC   5000BC   4000BC   3000BC

Mastering metal

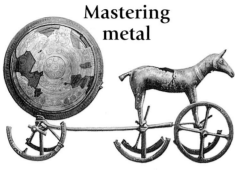

Gold and bronze model of the Sun on a horse-drawn chariot

Some people in Europe were using copper over 6000 years ago. Later, people learned how to make bronze by mixing copper with tin. Bronze weapons and tools were much harder than copper ones, and were very valuable.

Trading for tin

The tin needed to make bronze was only found in a few places in Europe (see map), so most people had to trade for it. The people of Scandinavia traded amber from the shores of the Baltic Sea for the metals they needed.

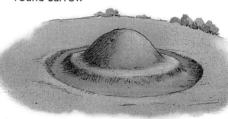

Bronze figure from Scandinavia

Tombs and treasure

The monument builders believed in life after death, and buried people with the weapons and tools they would need in the Next World. The tombs of wealthy people were filled with bronze swords and daggers, as well as beautiful golden objects.

Golden cup

A tomb called a round barrow

Important people were buried in round stone tombs covered with a great mound of earth. Each tomb held just one body. These tombs, called round barrows, are often found near stone circles.

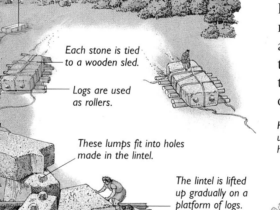

The stones are dragged from a quarry 32km (20 miles) away.

Each stone is tied to a wooden sled.

Logs are used as rollers.

These lumps fit into holes made in the lintel.

The lintel is lifted up gradually on a platform of logs.

Layers of logs are slipped under the lintel one at a time.

Men stand on this platform to help put the lintel in place.

These men are digging a hole for the next stone.

Wooden lever

Digging tools are made of bone and deer antlers.

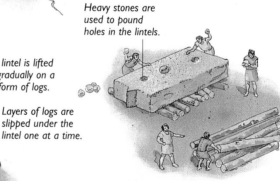

Heavy stones are used to pound holes in the lintels.

Important dates

c.3200BC People in northwestern Europe begin building stone circles.

c.3000–1500BC Stonehenge is built.

c.2500BC Metalworkers in Europe make bronze.

EUROPE

Palaces and Legends

Wall painting of a Minoan woman

The Minoans lived on the island of Crete in the Mediterranean Sea. Their way of life slowly grew into the first great civilization in Europe. The Minoans take their name from King Minos, who is said to have ruled the island.

The legend of King Minos

According to a Greek legend, the god Zeus fell in love with a beautiful princess called Europa. He turned himself into a bull and swam to Crete with the princess on his back. King Minos of Crete was one of Princess Europa's sons.

This painting of Europa and Zeus is taken from a Greek vase.

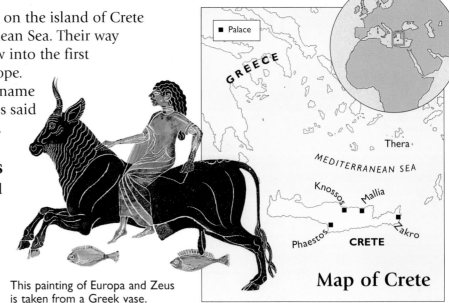

■ Palace

GREECE

Thera

MEDITERRANEAN SEA

Knossos Mallia

Phaestos CRETE Zakro

Map of Crete

The palace at Knossos

Each of the main towns on Crete was built around a huge palace, but the one at Knossos was the largest. It had over a thousand rooms, which were linked by corridors, staircases and courtyards.

Farmers bring grain to the palace storerooms.

The storerooms are at ground level.

Shafts like this let in the light.

Throne room

The roofs are made of wood.

The walls are built of limestone.

The central courtyard is used for religious ceremonies.

Wooden pillars hold up the roof.

The queen's bathroom

This picture shows the palace at Knossos. Part of the building has been cut away to let you see inside.

Storerooms

Farmers had to give some of their produce to the palace, where it was kept in the storerooms. Some of it was used to feed court officials and to pay the palace craftworkers. The rest was traded abroad.

Grain, oil and wine were stored in huge earthenware jars.

Painted walls

The palace walls were decorated with bright paintings called frescoes. A fresco is a picture which is painted on a wall while the plaster is still damp. The Minoans painted vivid scenes of palace life, plants and animals.

Fresco of a group of dolphins

The throne room

The king carried out ceremonies in the throne room. The throne in Knossos is made of stone and is the oldest throne in Europe still standing in its proper place. The walls are painted with frescoes of plants and mythical creatures, called griffins.

The throne room at Knossos

The legend of the Minotaur

According to legend, the Minotaur was half-bull and half-man, and lived in a huge maze under the palace at Knossos. A young Greek prince called Theseus set out to kill it. The daughter of King Minos gave Theseus a magic sword and a ball of thread. As he went deeper into the maze, Theseus unwound the thread, leaving a trail behind him. He used the sword to kill the monster and then followed the thread back to the outside world.

Theseus prepares to kill the Minotaur.

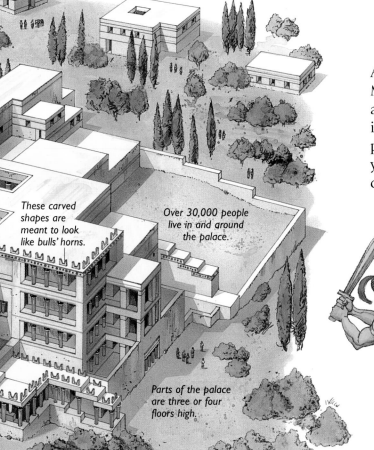

These carved shapes are meant to look like bulls' horns.

Over 30,000 people live in and around the palace.

Parts of the palace are three or four floors high.

EUROPE

| 2000BC | 1000BC | AD1 | AD500 |

Life on Crete

Most people on Crete were farmers. They kept animals, such as cattle, sheep, goats and pigs, and grew wheat, barley, vegetables, plums, grapes and olives. People also ate a lot of fish, which they caught in the sea around the island.

Wall painting of a fisherman holding his catch of mackerel

Travel and trade

The Minoans were skilled sailors. They had a large fleet of ships and sailed all around the eastern Mediterranean. Minoan merchants sold pottery, grain, wine and olive oil, and brought back gold, silver, jewels, ivory and linen. They were successful traders and became very rich.

Minoan pots

Writing

Once the Minoans began to store goods and trade with other lands, they needed to keep a record of who owned what. At first they used pictograms (picture writing), but later they invented a form of writing which experts call Linear A. So far, no one has been able to understand what it says.

Stone tablet carved with Linear A writing

This picture of a busy Minoan town gives an idea of what life on Crete was like.

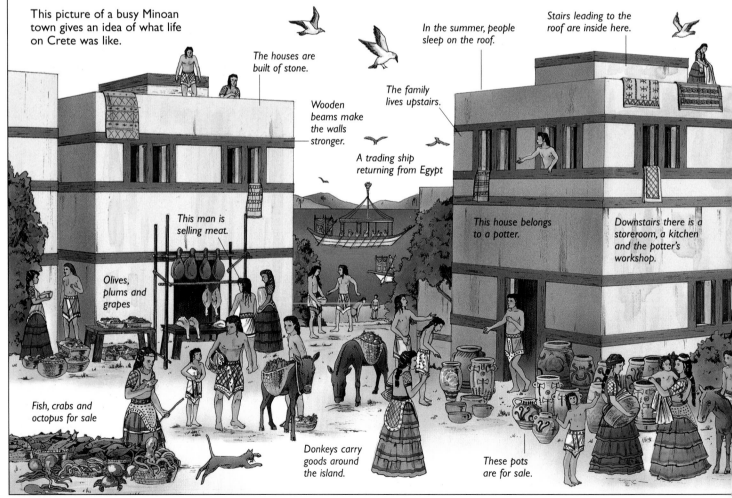

The houses are built of stone.

Wooden beams make the walls stronger.

A trading ship returning from Egypt

In the summer, people sleep on the roof.

The family lives upstairs.

Stairs leading to the roof are inside here.

This man is selling meat.

Olives, plums and grapes

This house belongs to a potter.

Downstairs there is a storeroom, a kitchen and the potter's workshop.

Fish, crabs and octopus for sale

Donkeys carry goods around the island.

These pots are for sale.

Bull-leaping

The Minoans enjoyed an extremely dangerous sport known as bull-leaping. Highly trained acrobats grasped the horns of a charging bull and somersaulted over its back. The bull was sacred to the sea god, so bull-leaping may have been part of a religious ceremony.

This wall painting shows a team of bull-leapers.

Religion

The Minoans did not build huge temples. Instead, they prayed and made offerings to their gods and goddesses in special rooms inside the palaces, or at small outdoor shrines.

Ash from the volcano on the island of Thera falls on Crete.

People try to escape as the buildings collapse.

An earthquake makes the palace walls crumble.

The end of the Minoans

Around 1450BC, there was a major disaster on Crete. The palaces were badly damaged, but no one is sure exactly how this happened. Around this time, a volcano on the nearby island of Thera erupted. This may have caused an earthquake or a giant tidal wave, which wrecked the Minoans' towns. Falling ash from the volcano may have ruined their farmland.

A disaster like the one shown here may have helped bring the Minoan civilization to an end.

At around the same time, Crete was invaded by people known as the Mycenaeans, who came from Greece (see pages 24 to 27). The Minoans never really recovered and their civilization gradually died out.

Shrine

These priestesses are going to worship at a shrine.

The double axe, a religious symbol

Statue of a goddess

Musicians

This calf will be sacrificed.

This priestess is carrying offerings of wine and oil.

Important dates

c.6000BC Farmers settle on Crete.

c.2500BC Towns begin to grow up.

c.1900BC The first palaces are built. Picture writing is used.

c.1700BC The palaces are destroyed by an earthquake.

c.1700-1450BC The palaces are rebuilt. Crete is at its most powerful.

c.1650BC Linear A writing is used.

c.1450BC The palaces are destroyed. The Mycenaeans invade. The Minoan civilization gradually dies out.

EUROPE

Palaces and Tombs

Wall painting of
a Mycenaean lady

Around 1600BC, the country now called Greece was divided into small kingdoms. Each kingdom was made up of a walled city and the land around it. The people who lived in Greece at this time became known as Mycenaeans, because Mycenae was the most important kingdom.

Mycenaean kings lived in magnificent palaces which contained offices, workshops and storerooms, as well as the king's private rooms. The most important room was the great hall, called the megaron.

Map of the Mycenaean world

This picture shows a feast in the megaron (great hall) of a Mycenaean palace.

The city of Mycenae

Palace

Windows up here let in
light and let out smoke.

The ceiling and floor
are brightly painted.

Wooden pillars
hold up the roof.

The king sits
on a raised
platform.

Roast
pig

Lyre

Circular fireplace

A poet sings about the
king's bravery in battle.

Pottery
drinking cup

Grapes and figs

Bread is eaten with
olive oil or honey.

This servant is
pouring out wine.

Workshops

Mycenaean pots

Metalworkers, potters and weavers worked for the king and had their workshops in the palace. Some of the things they made were traded abroad.

Offices

Scribes kept a record of all the goods stored in the palace. They wrote on clay tablets and used a form of writing which we call Linear B.

Clay tablet

Mycenaean scribes at work

Linear B writing

Bathrooms

One palace had a room with a built-in bathtub. The bathtub had no drain, so the water had to be scooped out with a jug and poured away.

Jar of perfumed oil

Stone bathtub

Stone step

The bathroom in the palace at Pylos

Early tombs

The early kings of Mycenae and their families were buried in deep pits, called shaft graves. The graves were protected by a circular stone wall.

A circle of graves at Mycenae

Each grave is marked by a stone slab.

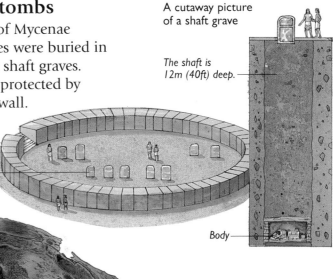

A cutaway picture of a shaft grave

The shaft is 12m (40ft) deep.

Body

Tomb treasure

Mycenaean tombs were filled with gold and silver ornaments, goblets, swords and daggers. Shaft graves were difficult for robbers to break into, so a lot of this treasure has survived.

This golden funeral mask was found in a shaft grave at Mycenae.

Beehive tombs

The later Mycenaean kings were buried in huge, beehive-shaped tombs, called tholos tombs. These tombs were built under great mounds of earth.

This cutaway picture of a tholos tomb shows a king's funeral.

Priests and priestesses bring offerings of food and wine.

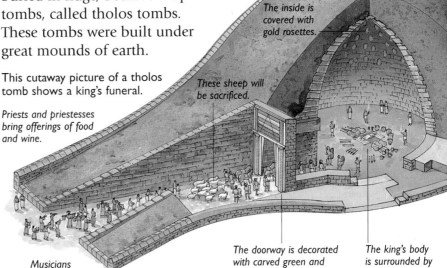

The inside is covered with gold rosettes.

These sheep will be sacrificed.

Musicians

The doorway is decorated with carved green and red stones.

The king's body is surrounded by treasure.

Warriors and Traders

War was an important part of Mycenaean life. Kings and nobles trained as warriors, skilled metalworkers made weapons from bronze, and poets told about the bravery of soldiers in battle.

Vase showing Mycenaean warriors

Hunting

When nobles were not at war, they used their chariots for hunting. They killed wild boar and used the tusks to decorate the helmets they wore in battle.

Hunting wild boar

When a city went to war, the king led his army into battle. He and his nobles rode in fast chariots, while the ordinary soldiers marched on foot.

In this picture, the king of the city of Mycenae is leading his army to war.

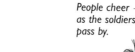

People cheer as the soldiers pass by.

This is the Lion Gate. It is the main entrance to Mycenae.

The city walls are built of huge blocks of stone.

Helmet covered with boars' tusks

Some warriors wear a bronze suit to protect them.

This huge rectangular shield is called a tower shield.

Some shields are shaped like a figure eight.

The chariots are made of wood and oxhide.

The king wears a helmet decorated with a horn.

Foot soldier

The shields are made of oxhide stretched over a wooden frame.

The invasion of Crete

Around 1450BC, Mycenaean warriors sailed to Crete and took control of the palace at Knossos. They also took over the Minoans' sea trade and became the leading traders in the eastern Mediterranean.

Mycenaean warships

Trade

Mycenaean traders sailed to places as far apart as Egypt and Italy. They bought ivory and precious metals in exchange for wine, olive oil, and objects such as weapons, pots and bowls.

This scene shows part of a busy Mycenaean trading port.

The siege of Troy

Around 1250BC, the city of Troy (in modern Turkey) was destroyed. A famous tale is told about this real event.

According to the legend, Paris, prince of Troy, fell in love with Helen, the beautiful wife of a Mycenaean king. Paris took Helen off to Troy, so the angry Mycenaeans attacked the city and kept it surrounded for ten years.

One day, they left a huge wooden horse outside the walls of Troy and pretended to sail away. The Trojans thought the horse would bring them luck and dragged it into the city.

Mycenaean soldiers climb out of the wooden horse.

That night, Mycenaean soldiers, who were hiding inside the horse, climbed out. They opened the city gates and let in the rest of their army. Troy was destroyed and Helen was reunited with her husband.

The end of the Mycenaeans

From around 1250BC, there were many bad harvests. Some of the Mycenaeans attacked each other's cities, and stole cattle and crops. Some may even have left Greece to search for new homes, and their cities were gradually abandoned.

Important dates

c.2000BC The Mycenaeans settle in Greece.

c.1600-1200BC The Mycenaeans are rich and powerful.

c.1450BC Knossos is taken over.

c.1250BC Troy is destroyed.

c.1200BC The cities are gradually abandoned.

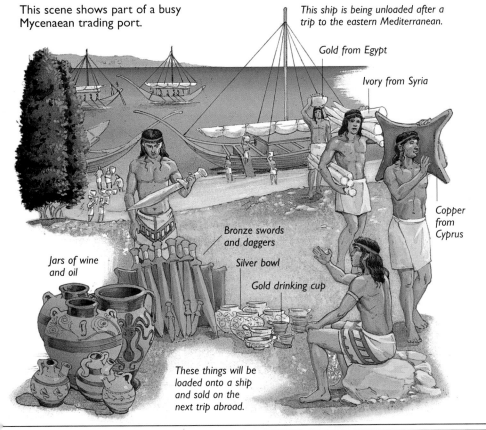

This ship is being unloaded after a trip to the eastern Mediterranean.

Gold from Egypt

Ivory from Syria

Copper from Cyprus

Bronze swords and daggers

Silver bowl

Gold drinking cup

Jars of wine and oil

These things will be loaded onto a ship and sold on the next trip abroad.

2000BC   1000BC   500BC   AD1   AD500

The Empire of Hammurabi

Map of Hammurabi's Empire

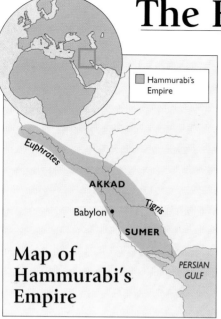

Euphrates

AKKAD

Babylon •

Tigris

SUMER

PERSIAN GULF

Hammurabi's Empire

Hammurabi's laws

Hammurabi put together one set of laws and punishments for all the people in his Empire. These laws were carved on a stone pillar for everyone to see.

These pictures show some of Hammurabi's laws.

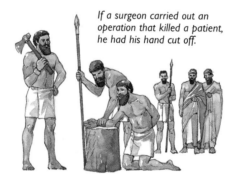

If a surgeon carried out an operation that killed a patient, he had his hand cut off.

If an architect built a house that collapsed and killed someone, he was put to death.

A man who owed money to someone could lend him his wife as a slave.

Gods and legends

Priests told how the god Marduk saved the world from a terrifying sea monster.

The Babylonians had many different gods, but Marduk was the most important one. Some people believed that Marduk created the world by building a huge raft on the ocean and pouring dust on top of it.

The end of the Empire

After Hammurabi died, his Empire grew weaker. Around 1595BC, the city of Babylon was raided by the Hittites, and the Empire collapsed. (To find out what happened in Babylon later on, see pages 46 and 47.)

Important dates

c.2000BC The Amorites invade.

c.1792-1750BC King Hammurabi rules Babylon and creates the Babylonian Empire.

c.1595BC The Hittites raid Babylon, and the Empire collapses.

Around 2000BC, the lands of Sumer and Akkad were invaded by desert tribes known as Amorites.

Amorite invaders

They took control of several cities, including Babylon. Each city was then ruled by a different Amorite family.

Around 1792BC, a young man called Hammurabi became King of Babylon. He fought the other Amorite kings and conquered the whole of Sumer and Akkad, creating a powerful empire.

This picture of King Hammurabi is based on a stone carving.

10,000BC   5000BC   4000BC   3000BC

The Hittite Empire

Map of the Hittite Empire

Hittite Empire

Hattushash

ANATOLIA

MITANNIAN EMPIRE

SYRIA

Qadesh

MEDITERRANEAN SEA

EGYPT

In around 2000BC, the Hittite people settled in Anatolia (in modern Turkey). By around 1650BC, they had all joined together to form one kingdom, with a capital city at Hattushash.

Kings and wars

The greatest Hittite king was Shuppiluliuma. He invaded Syria, destroyed the nearby Mitannian Empire and built up a powerful empire of his own.

The Hittites and the Egyptians were bitter enemies. They fought a fierce battle at Qadesh, which neither side won. The two countries later made peace.

Gold statue of a Hittite king

Gods

The Hittites had many gods, but their chief god was called Teshub. People believed that he controlled the weather.

Teshub holding a flash of lightning

The end of the Hittites

Around 1195BC, the Empire was attacked by raiders known as the Sea Peoples (see page 37). Some Hittites survived in Syria, but the Empire collapsed.

Warriors

The Hittites were tough warriors. They rode into battle in war chariots and carried iron weapons, which were stronger than the bronze weapons used by their enemies.

In this scene, Hittite warriors are leaving the city of Hattushash to go to war.

This gateway is called the Lion Gate.

Stone tower

There is a tunnel under the city wall, so soldiers can rush out and surprise the enemy.

City wall

Tunnel

The city is surrounded by a massive stone wall.

Iron helmet

Spear tipped with iron

This man drives the chariot.

Archers march on foot.

Wicker shield

Leather tunic covered with metal plates

The chariot is big enough to carry three men.

Important dates

c.2000BC The Hittites settle in Anatolia.

c.1650BC Hattushash is the capital of the Hittite kingdom.

c.1380-1340BC King Shuppiluliuma rules.

c.1285BC The Battle of Qadesh

c.1195BC The Hittites are defeated by the Sea Peoples.

The Egyptian Empire

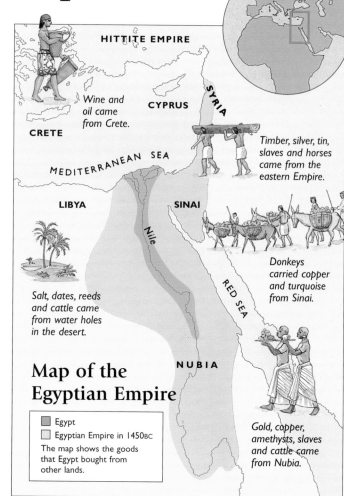

Around 1720BC, Egypt was invaded by people called the Hyksos. They had horses and chariots, and easily defeated the Egyptian soldiers who fought on foot. The Egyptians gradually learned how to use chariots and drove the Hyksos out of Egypt. Then, they began to invade nearby lands and quickly built up a large empire.

Egyptian painting showing a horse and chariot

Warrior pharaohs

The Egyptians were led into battle by their pharaohs (kings), who were skilled soldiers. The greatest warrior pharaoh was Tuthmosis III, who led his army to war 17 times. During his rule, the Egyptian Empire was at its largest.

The most dangerous of Egypt's enemies were the Hittites. Pharaoh Ramesses II fought against them for over 30 years. The two countries finally made peace, and Ramesses married a Hittite princess.

Map of the Egyptian Empire

HITTITE EMPIRE

Wine and oil came from Crete.

CYPRUS

SYRIA

CRETE

Timber, silver, tin, slaves and horses came from the eastern Empire.

MEDITERRANEAN SEA

LIBYA

SINAI

Nile

Donkeys carried copper and turquoise from Sinai.

Salt, dates, reeds and cattle came from water holes in the desert.

RED SEA

NUBIA

■ Egypt
□ Egyptian Empire in 1450BC
The map shows the goods that Egypt bought from other lands.

Gold, copper, amethysts, slaves and cattle came from Nubia.

Statue of Tuthmosis III

Trading trips

An Egyptian trading ship at Punt

Myrrh tree

The Egyptians had their own gold mines and could use the gold to buy the things they needed. They traded with other lands in their Empire and beyond (see map above). Some traders even went as far as Punt, a place on the east coast of Africa. There, they bought valuable myrrh trees, which were used to make sweet-smelling incense.

AFRICA

Paintings on the walls show scenes of life in Egypt.

Fan made of ostrich feathers

Pharaoh   Queen

Courtier

A scribe notes down the gifts people have brought.

Gifts of wine and oil for the pharaoh

Copper from Sinai

These Syrians are bowing very low.

One of the pharaoh's two viziers (advisers)

Officials

A herdsman from Sinai

Exotic fruit

Golden rings

Ostrich eggs

Ivory

Pet baboon for the queen

Visitors from Nubia

Leopard skin

In this scene, visitors are bringing gifts to the pharaoh's court. Some pillars have been taken out to show more of the throne room.

The pharaoh's court

People came from all over the Empire to the pharaoh's court. They brought goods to trade and rich gifts for the pharaoh. The gifts were a kind of tax, called tribute, that all conquered people had to pay. Some foreign rulers even sent their daughters to marry the pharaoh, who had many wives.

Travel

There were few roads in Egypt, as they would have been washed away by floods each year. The easiest way to travel was by boat along the Nile. Trading ships also sailed to ports on the Red Sea and in the eastern Mediterranean.

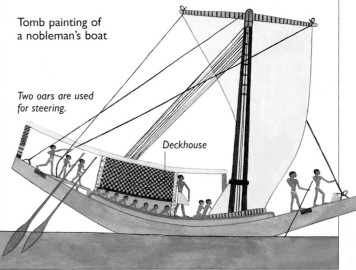

Tomb painting of a nobleman's boat

Two oars are used for steering.

Deckhouse

Temples and Gods

The Egyptians had many different gods and goddesses. Most of them were linked with a special animal or bird, and they were often shown in paintings and carvings with the head of that animal or bird. This made them easy to recognize.

Here you can see some Egyptian gods and goddesses.

Ma'at, goddess of truth and justice

Osiris, ruler of the dead

Taweret, a female hippopotamus, looked after pregnant women and babies.

Thoth, god of wisdom and writing, had the head of an ibis (a kind of bird).

Amun was king of the gods during the New Kingdom.

Re, the sun god, was sometimes shown with a hawk's head.

Anubis, god of the dead, had a jackal's head.

Horus, the son of Isis and Osiris, was god of the sky. He had a falcon's head.

Isis, the sister and wife of Osiris, was goddess of crafts.

Bast, the cat goddess

This temple at Abu Simbel in Nubia was carved out of solid rock.

The Egyptians built many huge, stone temples along the banks of the Nile. They believed that their gods and goddesses lived in these temples.

Inside each temple was a statue of the god who lived there. Every morning, priests woke the god, washed the statue, dressed it, gave it food and prayed to it.

Ordinary people did not normally go inside the temple. They only saw the statue of the god on festival days, when it was taken out and carried around the town.

This is the festival of Bast, the cat goddess. The procession is just leaving the temple.

Priests and priestesses lead the way.

This priest is burning incense.

These bulls will be sacrificed.

Golden boat

Statue of Bast

Shrine

Dancers   *Musicians*

Attached to the temple were craft workshops, a library and a school, and many different people worked there.

Some people who worked in the temple

Sculptor

Scribe (his job was to read and write for everyone else)

Carpenter

Potter

Weaver

Paper is very expensive, so the boys write on pieces of pottery.

The teacher is a scribe.

A temple school

A few boys from rich families went to the temple school to learn how to read and write. Older boys could study history, geography, religion, languages, mathematics and medicine. Girls did not go to school. They were taught at home by their mothers.

Writing

The Egyptians wrote in pictures or signs, which we call hieroglyphs. Scribes wrote on special paper, called papyrus, which was made from reeds. Ink was made in solid blocks and had to be mixed with water.

Papyrus

Block of ink

Wooden pens

This is a monument to the sun god. It is called an obelisk.

The temple walls are covered with carvings, paintings and hieroglyphs.

Hieroglyphs (picture writing)

Statue of the pharaoh (king)

Life at Home

Egyptian houses were built of bricks made from a mixture of mud and straw. The bricks were shaped in a wooden frame and were then left to dry in the sun. Most houses only had one or two rooms, but rich people lived in large, luxurious villas.

This huge villa belongs to a rich nobleman. He is receiving visitors in the reception hall. Part of the house has been cut away to let you see inside.

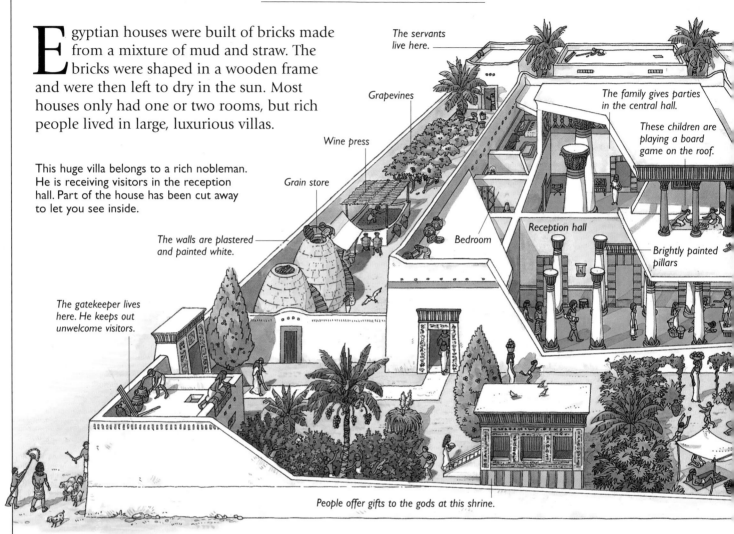

The servants live here.

Grapevines

Wine press

Grain store

The family gives parties in the central hall.

These children are playing a board game on the roof.

The walls are plastered and painted white.

Bedroom

Reception hall

Brightly painted pillars

The gatekeeper lives here. He keeps out unwelcome visitors.

People offer gifts to the gods at this shrine.

Parties

Rich Egyptians often gave large parties with lots of food and drink. Guests were entertained by musicians, singers, dancers, jugglers and acrobats. Servants put cones of perfumed fat on the guests' heads. As the fat melted and ran down their faces, it cooled them down and made them smell nice.

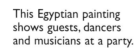

Perfumed fat

This Egyptian painting shows guests, dancers and musicians at a party.

Games

The Egyptians had several types of board games, such as the two shown on the right, but no one is sure how they were played. Children played with balls, spinning tops, dolls and animals made from wood or pottery.

Hounds and jackals

Senet

Toy dog

This handle opens the dog's mouth.

Hippo made of painted pottery

Clay balls

Cattle pens

Well

Fish pond

Shade to keep off the sun

Walled garden

The end of the Egyptian Empire

The last great warrior pharaoh was Ramesses III. He defended Egypt against raiders known as the Sea Peoples (see page 37).

After Ramesses died, the Empire grew weaker. Civil war broke out and Egypt was invaded by the Assyrians, then by the Nubians and later by the Persians.

In 332BC, Egypt was conquered by Alexander the Great (see pages 56 and 57). After Alexander's death, the country was ruled by the Ptolemy family, who were descended from one of his generals.

In 32BC, Rome went to war with Egypt. The Egyptians were defeated and Queen Cleopatra, the last Ptolemy ruler, killed herself. Egypt then became part of the Roman Empire.

Cleopatra

Sports

The most popular sports were hunting and fishing. Noblemen hunted water birds and river animals, such as hippos and crocodiles. People also enjoyed wrestling, fencing and energetic games, such as tug-of-war.

This picture of a tug-of-war comes from an Egyptian wall painting.

Hunting a hippo

Important dates

c.1720BC	The Hyksos invade Egypt. The Middle Kingdom ends.
c.1570BC	The Hyksos are driven out. The New Kingdom begins.
c.1450BC	The Egyptian Empire is at its largest.
c.1280BC	Ramesses II makes peace with the Hittites.
c.1190BC	The Sea Peoples attack.
c.1070BC	The New Kingdom ends in civil war.
671BC	The Assyrians invade.
525BC	The Persians invade.
332BC	Alexander the Great conquers Egypt.
30BC	Egypt becomes part of the Roman Empire.

AFRICA

2000BC   1000BC   500BC   AD1   AD500

The People of Canaan

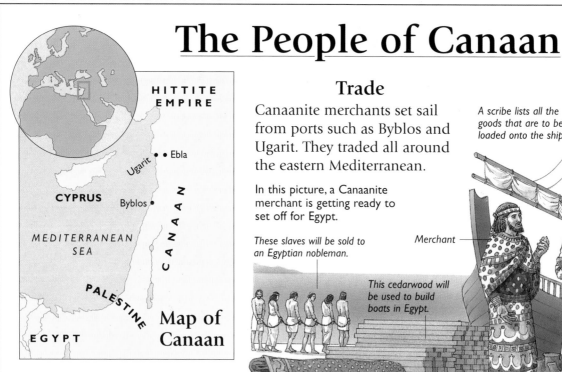

HITTITE EMPIRE

• Ebla

Ugarit •

CYPRUS

Byblos •

C A N A A N

MEDITERRANEAN SEA

PALESTINE

EGYPT

Map of Canaan

Trade

Canaanite merchants set sail from ports such as Byblos and Ugarit. They traded all around the eastern Mediterranean.

In this picture, a Canaanite merchant is getting ready to set off for Egypt.

A scribe lists all the goods that are to be loaded onto the ship.

These slaves will be sold to an Egyptian nobleman.

Merchant

This cedarwood will be used to build boats in Egypt.

Ivory box

Jar of olives

Brightly dyed cloth

Golden cups and vases

Jar of oil

Wine jars

T he land of Canaan lay at the eastern end of the Mediterranean Sea. The people of Canaan were farmers and traders, who lived in many small kingdoms. Each kingdom had a walled city with villages and farmland around it.

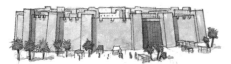

The city of Ebla

The huge cedar trees which grew in the north were very valuable, and Canaan became rich. It was fought over constantly by empire builders, such as the Egyptians and the Hittites. From around 1550BC, most of Canaan was ruled by Egypt.

Cedar tree

Gods

The Canaanites had many gods, but the most powerful one was Baal, the god of rain, storms and war. His wife, Astarte, was the goddess of love.

Statue of Baal

Priests sacrificed animals at hilltop shrines.

Writing

The Canaanites invented an alphabet with just 27 letters. It was much easier to use than Egyptian or Sumerian writing, which had hundreds of signs.

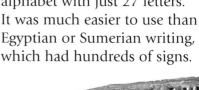

Clay tablet carved with Canaanite writing

Invasions

Between 1195BC and 1190BC, Canaan was invaded by the Sea Peoples (see opposite page). Some Sea Peoples settled in the south, but the Canaanites kept control in the north.

THE MIDDLE EAST

10,000BC   5000BC   4000BC   3000BC

36

Raiders of the Mediterranean

The Sea Peoples probably came from Greece, the Greek islands and southwestern Turkey. Around 1195BC, troubles at home forced them to look for somewhere else to live, and they invaded the eastern Mediterranean.

An army of Sea Peoples destroyed the Hittite Empire, then some of them sailed south, attacking towns on the coast of Canaan. Others made their way on foot, killing and destroying as they went.

Sea Peoples on the move

Women and children travel in carts.

Around 1190BC, the Sea Peoples attacked Egypt. They fought on land and sea, and were defeated in a fierce battle off the coast of Egypt.

This picture shows the sea battle between the Sea Peoples and the Egyptians.

The Philistines

After their defeat, the Sea Peoples scattered around the Mediterranean. One tribe, called the Peleset, settled in southern Canaan which was later named Palestine after them. In the Bible, they are known as Philistines.

The Philistines had strong iron weapons which helped them to conquer nearby tribes, such as the Hebrews (see pages 38 and 39).

Philistine coffins were made of pottery.

Egyptian archers fire arrows from the beach.

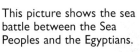

The Sea Peoples fight with spears or swords.

This tribe is called the Sherden. They wear helmets decorated with horns.

This ship has been overturned.

The Sea Peoples' ships have a bird's head at each end.

Leather tunic

The Egyptians fight with spears or bows and arrows.

The Egyptians ram one of the Sea Peoples' ships.

Many of the Sea Peoples are drowned.

Important dates

c.1550-1200BC Most of Canaan is ruled by the Egyptians.
c.1400BC The Canaanites invent the first alphabet.
c.1195BC The Sea Peoples defeat the Hittites.
c.1190BC The Egyptians defeat the Sea Peoples.
c.1150BC The Philistines settle in southern Canaan.

THE MIDDLE EAST

CANAANITES
SEA PEOPLES

| 2000BC | 1000BC | 500BC | AD1 | AD500 |

The Hebrew Kingdoms

The early Hebrews lived in tents.

The early Hebrew tribes wandered along the edges of the desert near the land of Canaan. Unlike most people in ancient times, they believed in only one god. They thought he would look after them if they obeyed him.

The great escape

You can read about the Hebrews in the Old Testament of the Bible. One famous story tells how they were forced to work for the kings of Egypt. Led by a man called Moses, they escaped across the desert into Canaan.

The Hebrews' escape from Egypt is known as the Exodus.

MEDITERRANEAN SEA

PHOENICIA

CANAAN

Jerusalem

EGYPT

Map of Israel

Kingdom of Israel at the time of David and Solomon

Philistine lands

Conquering Canaan

The Hebrews probably arrived in Canaan around 1250BC. After many battles, they won some land and settled down to farm.

This cutaway picture shows the house of a Hebrew farmer.

The roof is used as an extra room.

Olives, figs, dates and pomegranates grow in the orchard.

The family lives upstairs.

Oven for baking bread

Kneading dough

The animals are kept downstairs.

Crushing olives to make oil

Grain, oil and wine are stored in here.

Beans, lentils, garlic, onions and chickpeas are grown in the garden.

Goats are kept for meat and milk.

This woman is spinning wool.

This girl is going to get some water.

Fighting the Philistines

The Hebrews had to fight to defend their land against the Philistines who had settled on the coast. The Hebrews chose a man called Saul to be their king and lead them into battle, but the hero of the war was a boy called David. The Bible tells how he killed the Philistines' strongest warrior with a stone hurled from a sling.

David kills the Philistine warrior Goliath.

King David

David became king when Saul died. He defeated the Philistines and united the Hebrews into one kingdom, called Israel. He captured Jerusalem and made it his capital city.

THE MIDDLE EAST

King Solomon

David's son, Solomon, set up trade links with other lands, such as Phoenicia, and made Israel rich and powerful. He used part of his wealth to build a great temple in Jerusalem for his people's god.

This cutaway picture shows Solomon's temple in Jerusalem.

Outside Solomon's temple was a bronze basin filled with holy water.

Phoenician craftworkers helped the Hebrews to build the temple.

The temple is built of limestone.

The walls are lined with cedarwood from Phoenicia.

This room is called the Holy of Holies. The High Priest comes in here once a year.

The walls are covered with gold.

Porch

Bronze pillar

Storerooms for temple treasure

Main hall

Golden lampstand

Offerings of grain are burned on this altar.

This box is called the Ark of the Covenant. Inside it are stone slabs carved with sacred laws called the Ten Commandments.

The Ark is guarded by two golden statues.

Two kingdoms

After Solomon's death, quarrels broke out between the north and the south. The country split into two kingdoms, Israel in the north and Judah in the south.

The end of the Hebrew kingdoms

In 722BC, the Assyrians invaded Israel and took control. The Israelites later rebelled and many were taken to Assyria as slaves. Judah was conquered by the Babylonians, who destroyed Jerusalem and took the Judeans prisoner. The Judeans, who became known as Jews, were allowed to return home after the Babylonian Empire collapsed.

The people of Judah were taken to Babylon as slaves.

Important dates

c.1250BC	The Hebrews arrive in Canaan.
c.1020BC	Saul becomes king.
c.1000–965BC	King David rules. The Philistines are defeated.
c.965–928BC	King Solomon rules. The temple is built.
c.926BC	The kingdom splits in two, Israel and Judah.
722BC	The Assyrians invade Israel.
587BC	The Babylonians destroy Jerusalem. The people of Judah are taken prisoner.

| 2000BC | | 1000BC | 500BC | AD1 | AD500 |

Traders from Phoenicia

The Phoenicians were descended from the Canaanites, who lived at the eastern end of the Mediterranean Sea (see page 36). From around 1200BC, they became the most successful traders in the ancient world.

Crafts

Skilled craftworkers made objects for traders to sell abroad. The Phoenicians were known for their fine ivory carvings and their beautiful glass bottles and beads.

Glass bead

Ivory carving

Cities by the sea

The main Phoenician trading ports were the cities of Tyre, Sidon and Byblos. The cities were protected by strong walls and each one had its own king, who lived in a luxurious palace.

Purple people

The Phoenicians used a shellfish, called a murex, to make an expensive purple dye. The name "Phoenician" comes from a Greek word meaning "purple men".

Murex shell

A Phoenician city

Ships and sailing

The Phoenicians were expert sailors. Their sturdy trading ships sailed all over the Mediterranean and beyond, probably even reaching the British Isles. One expedition sailed all the way around Africa.

This picture shows a ship being loaded with cargo at a busy Phoenician trading port.

The ship is steered from the back using two huge oars.

This trading ship is about to set sail for Spain.

Cargo is stored below the deck.

Jars of cedar oil, wine and spices

Phoenician cedarwood

This merchant wants to buy some cloth.

Salt from North Africa

Ivory from Egypt

Copper from Cyprus

Rolls of purple cloth

Glass bottles are packed inside pottery jars to keep them safe.

Map of the Phoenician world

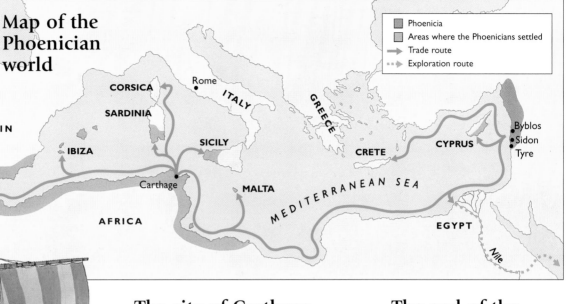

Phoenicia
Areas where the Phoenicians settled
Trade route
Exploration route

CORSICA
Rome
ITALY
GREECE
SARDINIA
SPAIN
SICILY
CYPRUS
Byblos
Sidon
Tyre
IBIZA
CRETE
TO THE BRITISH ISLES
Carthage
MALTA
MEDITERRANEAN SEA
TO WEST AFRICA
AFRICA
EGYPT
Nile

A warship sails ahead to protect trading ships from pirates.

A warship with two rows of oars is called a bireme.

The ship is made of cedarwood and pine.

This is the merchant who owns the ship.

The city of Carthage

Merchants set up trading posts and colonies around the Mediterranean. The most famous one was Carthage on the north coast of Africa. It was set up by a Phoenician princess called Dido, who tricked the local African ruler into giving her enough land to build a city.

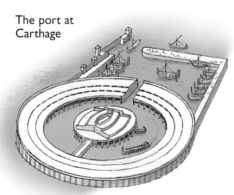

The port at Carthage

Writing

The Phoenicians invented a simple alphabet with just 22 letters. It gradually developed into the alphabet we use today.

Part of the Phoenician alphabet

Phoenician letters	B	Y	L	W	N	Φ
Modern letters	H	K	L	M	N	Q

The end of the Phoenicians

Although the Phoenicians became part of the mighty empires of Assyria, Babylon and Persia, their way of life survived until they were conquered by Alexander the Great in 332BC. The city of Carthage remained powerful for another 200 years, but was totally destroyed by the Romans in 146BC.

Roman soldiers destroying Carthage

Important dates

c.1200-1000BC The Phoenicians become rich and powerful.

c.814BC Carthage is built.

c.701BC Phoenicia is conquered by the Assyrians.

332BC Phoenicia is conquered by Alexander the Great.

146BC Carthage is destroyed by the Romans.

2000BC   1000BC   500BC   AD1   AD500

THE MIDDLE EAST

The Assyrians at War

In early times, the Assyrians lived in a small area of farmland by a river called the Tigris. Around 2000BC, they were taken over by invaders who made Assyria into a kingdom.

The Assyrians were warlike people. They often attacked the surrounding lands, but were always beaten back. Finally, led by a series of strong kings, they conquered the nearby kingdoms and built up a huge empire.

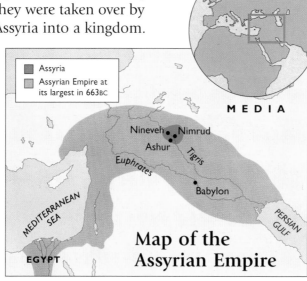

Assyria

Assyrian Empire at its largest in 663BC

MEDIA

Nineveh • Nimrud
Ashur •
Euphrates
Tigris
Babylon •

MEDITERRANEAN SEA

PERSIAN GULF

EGYPT

Map of the Assyrian Empire

Cruel conquerors

Conquered people had to pay heavy taxes to the Assyrian king, and anyone who refused to pay was brutally punished. Cities that rebelled were attacked.

The man in this carving is paying his taxes by giving a camel.

Attacking a city

The Assyrians were experts at attacking cities. They kept the city surrounded, so no one could escape. Then, they battered down the walls and captured the city.

In this scene, the Assyrians are attacking a rebel city.

A messenger brings news of a rebellion in another city.

Going to war

Every year, the mighty Assyrian army set out to conquer new lands. Soldiers had to travel great distances before going into battle.

This picture shows the Assyrian army crossing a river.

Chariots are rowed across in small boats.

Most of the army is made up of foot soldiers.

Soldiers swim across holding onto inflated goatskins.

Shield-bearer

Archer

Driver

Each chariot carries three soldiers.

These soldiers are blowing up goatskins to make floats.

The rebels throw flaming torches at the Assyrians.

Rebel soldiers try to push the ladders away.

Assyrian soldiers use ladders to climb up the walls.

This machine is called a siege engine.

Archers fire arrows through these holes.

Archers fire arrows high over the walls.

Covering made of animal skins

A battering ram breaks down the wall.

The Assyrians have built a ramp so they can attack the wall high up where it is weaker.

Soldiers dig under the wall to make it collapse.

Soldiers push the siege engine from behind.

Slingers hurl stones at the rebels.

Punishing rebels

Often, a captured city was destroyed and its people were taken prisoner or killed. Many were tortured to death. The Assyrians hoped this would teach other cities not to rebel, but instead it made them even more unpopular.

This picture shows Assyrian soldiers destroying a captured city.

Houses in the city are set on fire.

Soldiers knock down the city walls.

Orchards are burned.

Rebels are killed.

A scribe counts the heads of dead citizens.

Prisoners are led away.

The king's shield-bearer

The king gives orders from his chariot.

The king's guards

Tunic made of metal plates

| 2000BC | | 1000BC | 500BC | AD1 | AD500 |

The Assyrians at Home

Most people in Assyria were farmers. They dug ditches to carry water to their fields and grew barley, sesame, grapes and vegetables. Farmers also kept sheep, goats and cattle.

Wooden pole

Stone weight

Leather bucket

A machine called a shaduf lifts water into the fields.

An Assyrian farmer at work

Gods and spirits

The Assyrians believed that their land belonged to Ashur, their chief god. They had many other gods and goddesses, and also believed in evil spirits.

Mighty kings

Assyrian kings thought that they were chosen by the gods to rule Assyria and conquer new lands. They gave themselves grand titles, such as "King of the Universe". The king also served the gods by building temples and leading religious festivals.

Statue of King Ashurnasirpal II

Cities and palaces

The Assyrians built magnificent cities with beautiful palaces and temples. Their first capital city at Ashur was named after their god. Later, King Ashurnasirpal II built a new capital city at Nimrud.

The throne room in Ashurnasirpal's palace at Nimrud

An opening in the ceiling lets in light.

The statue has a human head and the body of a winged lion.

A messenger brings news from around the Empire.

This is one of the two statues that guard the entrance to the throne room.

A servant holds a canopy over the king.

A scribe takes notes.

By the time of Ashurbanipal, the last great Assyrian king, the capital had been moved to another new city at Nineveh.

This picture shows King Ashurbanipal and his queen in the palace garden at Nineveh.

Double flute

Harp

The king's dogs

Lotus flowers grow in the pool.

Musicians

4000BC

3000BC

Libraries

An Assyrian library

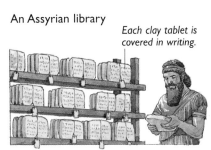

Each clay tablet is covered in writing.

The palace at Nineveh had a library filled with hundreds of clay tablets, which King Ashurbanipal collected from around the Empire. There were tablets on history, religion, mathematics and medicine.

Lion hunting

When Assyrian kings were not at war, they hunted lions to show off their skill and bravery. The lions were kept in special parks so that the king could hunt whenever he wanted.

King Ashurbanipal in his hunting park

Soldiers use their shields to stop the lions from escaping.

The king is about to kill a lion with his spear.

The lions are kept in cages.

Grapevines keep off the sun.

Servants fan the king and queen to keep them cool and chase away flies.

Cakes made of honey and figs

The king lies on a couch.

Burning incense perfumes the air.

The furniture is decorated with gold and ivory.

The end of the Empire

In the end, the Assyrian Empire became too big to control. People rebelled and the Empire began to break up. In 612BC, the people of Babylon and nearby Media joined together to attack Assyria. The cities of Ashur and Nineveh were completely destroyed and the Empire collapsed.

Median soldier

Important dates

c.2000BC   Assyria becomes a kingdom.

c.1000-663BC   The Assyrians build up a powerful empire.

883-859BC   King Ashurnasirpal II rules. Nimrud is built.

704-681BC   King Sennacherib builds the city of Nineveh.

668-627BC   King Ashurbanipal rules.

612-609BC   The Babylonians and the Medes attack Assyria. The Empire collapses.

THE MIDDLE EAST

The City of Babylon

Pottery head of a
Kassite priestess

Babylon first became powerful under its great king, Hammurabi (see page 28). When his Empire collapsed, the city was taken over by a tribe called the Kassites, who ruled peacefully for over 400 years.

After around 730BC, Babylon became part of the Assyrian Empire. The people of Babylon often rebelled against the Assyrians, who eventually attacked and destroyed the city.

In 625BC, a Babylonian general called Nabopolassar made himself King of Babylon. He joined with the people of nearby Media to defeat the Assyrians. He and his son, King Nebuchadnezzar II, rebuilt Babylon and made it one of the richest cities in the world.

This picture shows the city of Babylon during the New Year Festival.

This gateway is called the Ishtar Gate. It is named after the goddess Ishtar.

The gate is covered with bright blue tiles.

This stepped tower is called a ziggurat. It was built by Nebuchadnezzar for the god Marduk.

Shrine

Priests live here.

The king's throne room

The king's palace

These gardens are known as the Hanging Gardens of Babylon.

Nebuchadnezzar built the gardens for his wife, because she missed the green hills of her homeland.

An avenue called the Processional Way leads into the city.

Pictures of bulls and dragons

A statue of the god Marduk is carried to a shrine outside the city.

People watch the procession from the battlements.

10,000BC   5000BC   4000BC   3000BC

Map of the Babylonian Empire

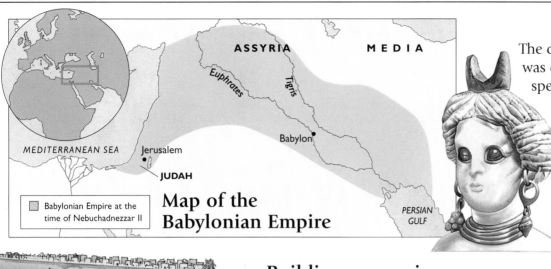

ASSYRIA   MEDIA

Euphrates

Tigris

Babylon

MEDITERRANEAN SEA

Jerusalem

JUDAH

PERSIAN GULF

Babylonian Empire at the time of Nebuchadnezzar II

Religion

The chief god of Babylon was called Marduk. His special festival was the New Year Festival which lasted 11 days. The chief goddess was Ishtar, the goddess of love and war.

Statue of the goddess Ishtar

Building an empire

King Nebuchadnezzar II fought many wars and built up a large empire. One of his most famous wars was against the people of Judah. When they rebelled, he destroyed Jerusalem, their capital city, and took thousands of them to Babylon as slaves.

Machinery carries water to the top of the Hanging Gardens.

Water runs down the terraces and keeps the soil wet.

Telling the future

The Babylonians believed that they could tell the future by looking at the insides of dead animals. Priests had clay models which showed them what to look for.

Clay model of a sheep's liver

The end of Babylon

In 539BC, Babylon was captured by an army from Persia (modern Iran) and became part of the powerful Persian Empire (see pages 48 and 49).

The main part of the city is surrounded by two massive walls.

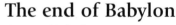

Important dates

c.1595–1155BC	The Kassites rule Babylon.
c.730BC	Babylon becomes part of the Assyrian Empire.
689BC	Babylon is destroyed.
625–605BC	King Nabopolassar rules. The Assyrians are defeated.
605–562BC	King Nebuchadnezzar II rules. Babylon is rebuilt.
539BC	Babylon becomes part of the Persian Empire.

2000BC   1000BC   500BC   AD1   AD500

The Power of Persia

Persia is the old name for the country we now call Iran. Around 1300BC, the area was invaded by two tribes known as the Medes and the Persians. They set up two kingdoms, Media in the north and Persia in the south.

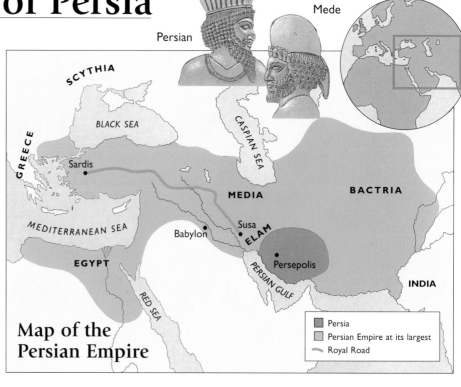

Mede

Persian

Map of the Persian Empire

- Persia
- Persian Empire at its largest
- Royal Road

SCYTHIA
BLACK SEA
GREECE
CASPIAN SEA
Sardis
MEDITERRANEAN SEA
MEDIA
BACTRIA
Babylon
Susa
ELAM
EGYPT
Persepolis
PERSIAN GULF
RED SEA
INDIA

Frieze showing Persian soldiers

In 550BC, King Cyrus II of Persia defeated the Medes, took over their lands and built up a huge empire. Later, under King Darius I, the Persian Empire grew to become the largest the world had ever seen.

The Royal Road

Darius built good roads across the Empire, so that messengers could travel more quickly. The Royal Road stretched 2700km (1680 miles) from Sardis in the west to the capital city at Susa.

Persian armlet made of solid gold

Running the Empire

King Darius collected taxes from conquered people all over the Empire and became fabulously rich. He allowed people to keep their religion and way of life, as long as they paid their taxes.

Darius divided his vast Empire into regions, each one run by a local ruler called a satrap. Officials kept an eye on the satraps and made sure they stayed loyal to the king.

A messenger arrives at an inn along the Royal Road.

Canopy

This picture shows King Darius receiving visitors in his throne room.

Officials

Burning incense perfumes the air.

Prince Xerxes, the king's son

King Darius

A satrap (local ruler) greets the king.

Guards

Persepolis

Darius used some of his wealth to build a magnificent palace at Persepolis. During the New Year Festival, officials from every part of the Empire came to the palace with gifts for the king.

This picture shows people arriving at Persepolis for the New Year Festival.

This is the Great Hall, where the king receives his visitors. It can hold 10,000 people.

The tops of the pillars are carved in the shape of bulls.

Inside, the Great Hall is decorated with gold, silver, ivory and ebony (a dark wood).

Staircase covered with carvings

This man has brought a camel from Bactria.

An African carrying ivory

Visitors wait outside in the courtyard.

Persian officials

A Scythian brings cloth and a golden armlet.

This Indian is carrying pots of gold dust.

A Babylonian with gifts of gold and silver bowls

A Mede shows people where to wait.

Guards

This man is from Elam. He has brought a lion cub for the king.

Religion

The Persians followed the teachings of a prophet called Zarathustra (or Zoroaster), who taught that there was only one god. Fire was holy, and priests (called Magi) kept a sacred fire burning.

Priests carried twigs to feed the sacred fire.

The end of the Persian Empire

For many years, Persia was at war with Greece. The Persians won some battles, but were eventually beaten back. (You can find out more about these wars on page 51.)

After the death of Darius's son, King Xerxes I, the Empire grew weaker. In 331BC, Persia was conquered by Alexander the Great (see pages 56 and 57).

Important dates

c.1300BC	The Medes and the Persians settle down.
c.700-600BC	The kingdoms of Persia and Media are set up.
559-530BC	Cyrus II rules Persia.
550BC	Cyrus defeats the Medes.
522-486BC	Darius I rules Persia. The Empire is at its largest.
490-479BC	The Persians are at war with Greece.
486-465BC	Xerxes I rules Persia.
331-330BC	Persia is conquered by Alexander the Great. Persepolis is burned.

THE MIDDLE EAST

The Greeks at War

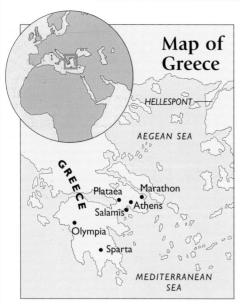

Map of Greece

HELLESPONT

AEGEAN SEA

GREECE

Plataea
Marathon
Athens
Salamis
Olympia
Sparta

MEDITERRANEAN SEA

Soldiers and armies

All the city-states had their own army, and they were often at war with each other. Heavily armed foot soldiers, called hoplites, were the most important part of an army.

This picture shows a group of hoplites (foot soldiers) charging at the enemy.

Spear

Horsehair crest

Bronze helmet

Shield of bronze, wood and leather

Bronze and leather breastplate

Sword

Bronze leg guard (called a greave)

A Greek hoplite

Hoplites fight in closely packed rows. A block of soldiers is called a phalanx.

Flute music helps the men keep in step with each other.

Soldiers at the front lower their spears.

If this soldier is killed, the man behind him will take his place.

The soldiers are protected by a wall of overlapping shields.

After the Mycenaean civilization collapsed (see page 27), life in Greece was hard. People had to spend all their time growing food and forgot many of the skills they had learned, such as writing. This period of time is called the Greek Dark Ages.

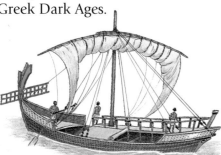

Greek trading ship

From around 800BC, the Greeks began to trade with other lands and became richer. They lived in small city-states with their own rulers and customs. Each city-state was made up of a city and the farmland around it. The two most important states were Athens and Sparta.

Sparta

The fiercest warriors in Greece came from Sparta. All Spartan men were full-time soldiers who spent their lives training and fighting.

Boys were taken from their mothers at the age of seven to begin their training. Girls had to keep fit, too, so that they would have strong, healthy babies.

Bronze statue of a Spartan warrior

Statue of a Spartan girl in a running race

The first marathon

In 490BC, the Persians invaded Greece. The Greeks fought back and defeated them in a fierce battle at Marathon. A runner carried the good news over 32km (20 miles) to Athens, and then died of exhaustion. The modern marathon race is named after this famous event.

The first marathon runner

The Persians fight back

In 480BC, the Persians attacked again. They built a bridge of boats tied together with ropes, and crossed the stretch of water known as the Hellespont. Then, they marched into Greece and destroyed the city of Athens.

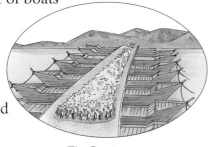

The Persian army crossing the Hellespont

Victory for Greece

The Greeks won a great sea battle near the island of Salamis. They trapped the Persian fleet in a narrow channel of water and wrecked over 200 Persian ships. The Greek army finally defeated the Persians in a huge land battle at Plataea.

This picture shows the sea battle between the Greeks and the Persians at Salamis.

A ship with three rows of oars is called a trireme. All the ships in this picture are triremes.

In a battle, the sail and mast are taken down and stored here.

This ship has been rammed and is sinking.

Each ship is rowed by 170 oarsmen.

The Persian ships are decorated with a dragon's head.

The ships are steered using two oars at the back.

Archers hide behind a row of shields.

Greek archer

Greek hoplites throw spears at the Persians.

A bronze ram smashes into the side of the Persian ship.

The painted eyes are meant to scare the enemy and help the ship see where it is going.

The Greek oarsmen row at full speed.

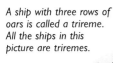

EUROPE

| 2000BC | | 1000BC | 500BC | AD1 | AD500 |

Life in Ancient Greece

Although the Greeks were almost always at war, they managed to create one of the greatest civilizations in history. The time from 500BC to 350BC is known as the Classical Period.

Life at home

While Greek men went out to work, shop and meet their friends, women stayed at home. They ran the household, looked after the children and supervised the slaves.

This picture shows a dinner party in the andron (dining room).

Musicians

Slaves serve the food.

Men wear a robe called a himation.

Slices of roast wild boar

Wine mixed with water

Barley bread

Fried octopus

The house in this cutaway picture belongs to a rich Greek family.

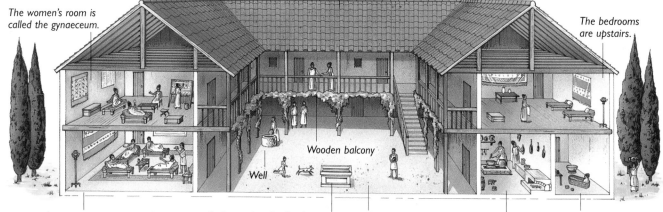

The roof is made of pottery tiles.

The women's room is called the gynaeceum.

The bedrooms are upstairs.

Wooden balcony

Well

The men eat in a room called the andron.

Each morning, the family meets for prayers around the altar.

Cobbled courtyard

The slaves are cooking dinner in the kitchen.

Bathroom with a terracotta bathtub

This picture shows women in the gynaeceum, where they spend most of their time.

Women weave tapestries to hang on the walls.

This girl is spinning wool.

Mirror

Jar of perfume

Women wear a robe called a chiton.

School

Boys from rich families started school when they were seven years old. They learned reading, writing, mathematics, music, poetry, athletics and dancing. Girls stayed at home and were taught by their mothers.

Vase painting of a boy learning to read

The Olympic Games

Athletics was a popular pastime for men in ancient Greece, and competitions were held all over the country. The most important was the Olympic Games. The Games were held every four years at Olympia, as part of a festival for Zeus, the king of the gods.

Discus thrower

Horse race

The main events at the Olympic Games were running, jumping, boxing, wrestling, horse racing, chariot racing, discus and javelin throwing. In one race, men had to run wearing a bronze helmet and leg guards and carrying a heavy shield.

Athlete with helmet, shield and leg guards

Drama

The first great plays in the world were written by the ancient Greeks. The plays were performed as part of religious festivals to please the gods. These festivals lasted several days and there was a prize for the best play.

This picture shows a play being performed.

Greek actors wore painted masks to show what sort of character they were playing.

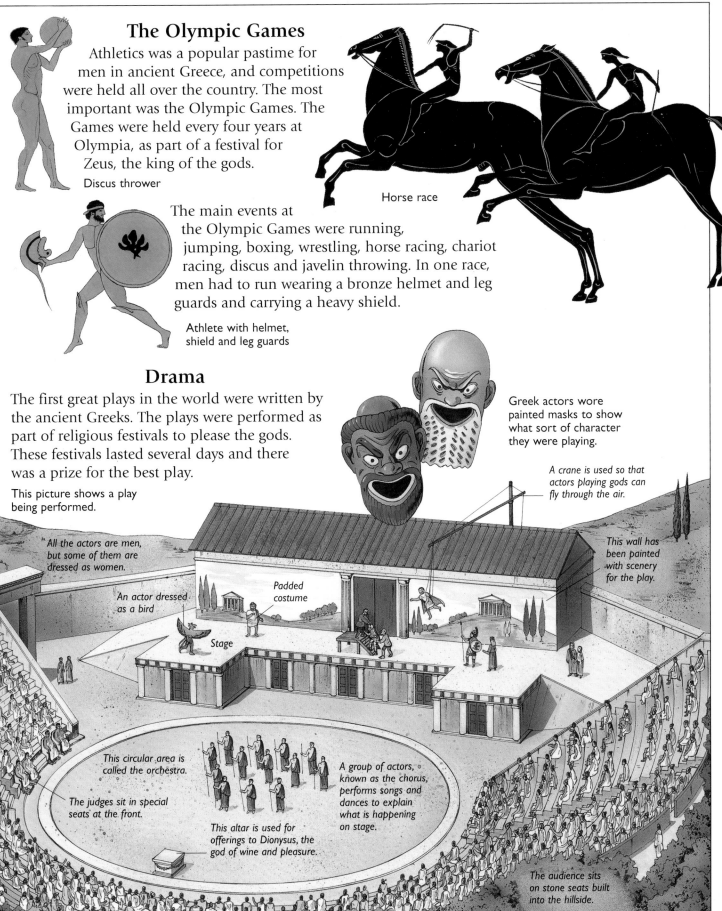

A crane is used so that actors playing gods can fly through the air.

All the actors are men, but some of them are dressed as women.

This wall has been painted with scenery for the play.

An actor dressed as a bird

Padded costume

Stage

This circular area is called the orchestra.

A group of actors, known as the chorus, performs songs and dances to explain what is happening on stage.

The judges sit in special seats at the front.

This altar is used for offerings to Dionysus, the god of wine and pleasure.

The audience sits on stone seats built into the hillside.

The City of Athens

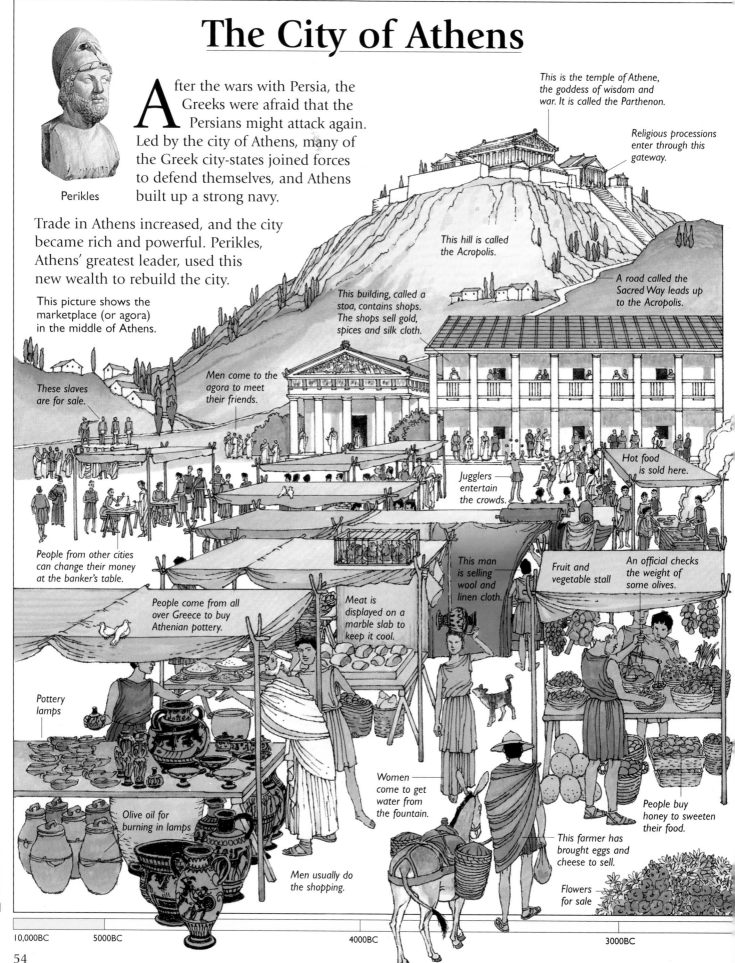

Perikles

After the wars with Persia, the Greeks were afraid that the Persians might attack again. Led by the city of Athens, many of the Greek city-states joined forces to defend themselves, and Athens built up a strong navy.

Trade in Athens increased, and the city became rich and powerful. Perikles, Athens' greatest leader, used this new wealth to rebuild the city.

This picture shows the marketplace (or agora) in the middle of Athens.

This is the temple of Athene, the goddess of wisdom and war. It is called the Parthenon.

Religious processions enter through this gateway.

This hill is called the Acropolis.

A road called the Sacred Way leads up to the Acropolis.

This building, called a stoa, contains shops. The shops sell gold, spices and silk cloth.

These slaves are for sale.

Men come to the agora to meet their friends.

Hot food is sold here.

Jugglers entertain the crowds.

People from other cities can change their money at the banker's table.

This man is selling wool and linen cloth.

Fruit and vegetable stall

An official checks the weight of some olives.

People come from all over Greece to buy Athenian pottery.

Meat is displayed on a marble slab to keep it cool.

Pottery lamps

Olive oil for burning in lamps

Women come to get water from the fountain.

Men usually do the shopping.

This farmer has brought eggs and cheese to sell.

People buy honey to sweeten their food.

Flowers for sale

EUROPE

10,000BC   5000BC   4000BC   3000BC

54

Power to the people

In Athens, all free men had a say in how the city was run. They met once every ten days to discuss new laws, and took decisions by voting. This type of government is called democracy, which means "rule by the people". Women, foreigners and slaves were not allowed to vote.

A politician making a speech to the men of Athens

Beautiful buildings

The Greeks built magnificent temples from gleaming white marble. Most temples had a triangular-shaped roof held up by rows of columns (pillars). All over the world, people have copied the style of Greek buildings.

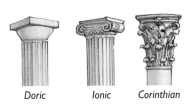

Doric   Ionic   Corinthian

Greek columns were built in three different styles.

The Parthenon in Athens is a typical Greek temple.

Science and learning

Plato

Socrates

Greek thinkers asked themselves questions about how people should behave. Two of the most famous, Socrates and Plato, lived in Athens.

Scientists tried to explain how the world worked. They studied plants, animals, the human body, the Sun and the stars.

One astronomer found out that the Earth moves around the Sun.

Scholars, such as Pythagoras, discovered rules that are still used in mathematics today.

Manuscript showing Pythagoras' ideas about triangles

A Greek called Herodotus wrote the first proper history book in the world. It was about the Persian Wars.

Herodotus interviewed survivors of the Persian Wars.

War with Sparta

Some of the Greek city-states grew worried that Athens had become too powerful and, in 431BC, war broke out between Athens and Sparta. The other city-states joined in, and the war (called the Peloponnesian War) lasted 27 years. Athens was finally defeated, but all the city-states were left weak and exhausted.

Vase painting of Greek soldiers

EUROPE

2000BC   1000BC   500BC   AD1   AD500

Alexander the Great

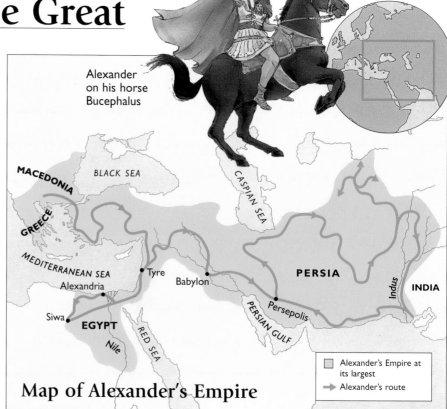

Alexander on his horse Bucephalus

Map of Alexander's Empire

MACEDONIA

GREECE

BLACK SEA

CASPIAN SEA

MEDITERRANEAN SEA

Tyre

Babylon

PERSIA

Alexandria

Siwa

EGYPT

RED SEA

Nile

PERSIAN GULF

Persepolis

Indus

INDIA

☐ Alexander's Empire at its largest
→ Alexander's route

The Greek city-states kept on fighting each other even after the Peloponnesian War was over. They were too busy to see what was happening in the kingdom of Macedonia to the north.

King Philip II of Macedonia

The Macedonian king, Philip II, had built up a strong army of well-trained soldiers. He began to conquer the Greek city-states and, by 338BC, he controlled all of Greece. Soon after this, Philip was murdered and his 20-year-old son, Alexander, became king.

Alexander's conquests

Alexander was a brave soldier and a brilliant commander. He led his army on a journey of over 32,000km (almost 20,000 miles), creating the largest empire in the ancient world. Today, he is known as Alexander the Great.

Mosaic showing Alexander in battle

1 Alexander attacked the port of Tyre, using rocks fired from catapults on boats. It took months to capture the city.

3 The Persians were defeated by Alexander in 331BC. His army later captured the palace of Persepolis and set it on fire.

2 The Egyptians welcomed Alexander. At Siwa, a desert oasis, he was greeted as the son of the Egyptian god Amun.

4 In India, Alexander defeated a king called Porus, whose army rode on hundreds of war elephants.

Alexandria

Alexander built new Greek-style cities all over his Empire and named many of them after himself. The most famous is Alexandria in Egypt. Scholars came to Alexandria from all over the Greek world to study and discuss new ideas. Many things were invented there, including the first lighthouse in the world.

This picture shows the lighthouse at Alexandria.

The lighthouse, known as the Pharos, was one of the seven wonders of the ancient world.

Statue of Zeus, king of the gods

A fire is kept burning at the top.

Bronze mirrors reflect the light. It can be seen 50km (30 miles) away.

Carts filled with wood for the fire are pulled up a ramp inside the lighthouse.

The second level has eight sides.

The first level has four sides.

Inside are rooms for the lighthouse workers and guards.

A causeway links the lighthouse to the mainland.

The base is built of massive stone blocks. The rest is made of marble.

A trading ship returning from the Black Sea

Alexander's death

Alexander had to return from India because his exhausted troops refused to go any farther. Soon after reaching Babylon, he caught a fever and died. He was just 33 years old.

Statue of Alexander wearing a lion skin

After Alexander

After Alexander's death, his generals fought each other for control of the Empire. Antigonas took Greece and Macedonia. Ptolemy won Egypt, where his family ruled for the next 300 years. The rest was taken by Seleucus and became known as the Seleucid Empire. In the end, all three kingdoms were conquered by the Romans.

Egyptian carving of Ptolemy

Important dates

c.1100-800BC	The Greek Dark Ages
c.776BC	The first Olympic Games
c.508BC	Democracy begins in Athens.
490-479BC	The Persian Wars
461-429BC	Perikles leads Athens.
447-438BC	The Parthenon is built.
431-404BC	The Peloponnesian War
338BC	Philip II of Macedonia takes control of Greece.
336-323BC	Alexander rules Greece and builds up his Empire.
323-281BC	Alexander's generals fight. The Empire splits up.
146BC	Greece becomes part of the Roman Empire.

EUROPE

2000BC   1000BC   500BC   AD1   AD500

Riders of the Plains

Among the many tribes who roamed across the plains of central Asia was a tribe of horsemen known as the Scythians. By around 700BC, they had moved into the land north of the Black Sea, conquering the people who lived there.

Scythian horseman

Map of the Scythian world

BLACK SEA

GREECE

PERSIAN EMPIRE

MEDITERRANEAN SEA

☐ Scythian lands
■ Areas where the Greeks settled

Scythians in battle

Bloody battles

Scythian warriors were skilled at fighting on horseback. They were excellent archers, but also fought with spears and battle-axes. After a battle, they used the skulls of their dead enemies to make drinking cups.

Life on the move

The Scythians bred horses and kept herds of cattle and sheep. They were nomads (wandering people) who were always on the move, looking for grass where their animals could graze. They lived in tents which they could pack up and carry with them.

In this picture of a Scythian camp, one tent has been cut away to let you see inside.

This slave is an Assyrian soldier who was captured in battle.

The tents are made of felt.

The larger tents have two or three rooms inside.

This girl is doing embroidery.

Carved wooden table

The inside is lined with bright wall hangings.

This woman is cooking a beef stew.

Carpets and cushions make the tent comfortable.

Copper cooking pot

This boy is drinking horse's milk.

Bowls are made of leather, clay or wood.

This woman is sewing felt shapes onto cloth to make a wall hanging.

Dead and buried

When a Scythian chief died, he was buried with his most precious possessions under a huge mound (called a kurgan). A year later, 50 men and horses were killed and placed around the mound.

This scene shows the funeral procession of a Scythian chief.

A mound (or kurgan) like this will be built over the chief's tomb.

Golden comb from a Scythian tomb

The horses wear elaborate headdresses.

Golden harness

These servants will be sacrificed so they can serve the chief in the Next World.

The chief's horses will be killed and buried with him.

The chief's body is covered with golden rings, bracelets and necklaces.

The chief's wife

People shave their heads and cut themselves to show their grief.

This man is about to cut off his ear.

Wealth and weakness

The Scythians sold wheat grown by farmers whose lands they had conquered. They traded with the Greeks and bought precious metals from merchants in central Asia. They also taxed traders passing through their lands and became very rich.

Around 300BC, the Scythians' power began to weaken, and they were eventually conquered by King Mithridates who ruled the land south of the Black Sea.

The men use horses to round up their cattle and sheep.

This boy is learning to use a bow and arrow.

In the winter, people wear warm clothes made of wool, fur, felt or leather.

Sheepskin coat

These men are going hunting for deer and hares.

Quiver containing arrows

This man is making leather from animal skins.

This man is making a new bow.

Important dates

c.700-600BC	Scythian warriors raid nearby lands.
514BC	The Scythians fight off an attack by the Persians.
c.400-300BC	The Scythians are rich and successful.
110-106BC	The Scythians are defeated.

EUROPE

2000BC   500BC   AD1   AD500

The People of Early China

Area ruled by the Shang kings

Yellow

YELLOW SEA

Yangtze

Early Chinese pot

Map of China

China is surrounded by mountains, deserts and seas, and for thousands of years it was cut off from the rest of the world. The way of life that grew up there was quite different from life anywhere else in the ancient world.

The first farmers

Around 5000BC, people began farming along the banks of the Yellow River. They grew millet (a type of grain), fruit, nuts and vegetables, and kept pigs, dogs and chickens. Along the Yangtze River, where it was warmer and wetter, people grew rice.

A farmer planting rice shoots

The first Chinese farmers built villages, used stone tools for working in the fields and made beautiful painted pots.

This picture shows an early Chinese farming village. Part of one house has been cut away to let you see inside.

Silk and silkworms

Cocoon

The cocoons are rinsed in hot water to loosen the threads.

A woman blows on the fire to keep it hot.

A silkworm feeding on a mulberry leaf

Unwinding thread from silk cocoons

Silk thread is made by silkworms (a type of caterpillar), who spin it into cocoons to protect themselves while they turn into moths. The Chinese were the first to learn how to unwind the thread from the cocoons and spin it into fine silk cloth.

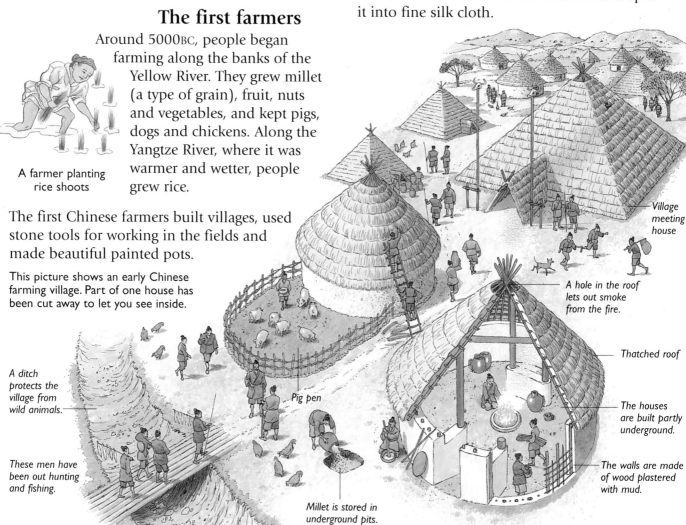

Village meeting house

A hole in the roof lets out smoke from the fire.

Thatched roof

The houses are built partly underground.

A ditch protects the village from wild animals.

Pig pen

These men have been out hunting and fishing.

The walls are made of wood plastered with mud.

Millet is stored in underground pits.

10,000BC   5000BC   4000BC   3000BC

The Shang kings

By around 1765BC, a large part of China was ruled by a family (or dynasty) of kings called the Shang. When a king died, he was buried in a huge pit filled with precious objects. People and animals were sacrificed and placed in the pit with him.

This scene shows the funeral ceremony of a Shang king.

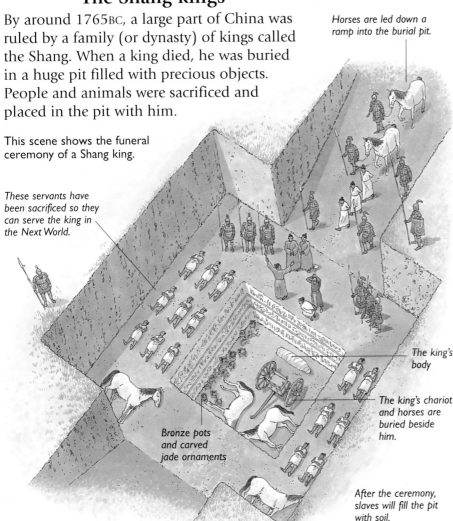

Horses are led down a ramp into the burial pit.

These servants have been sacrificed so they can serve the king in the Next World.

Bronze pots and carved jade ornaments

The king's body

The king's chariot and horses are buried beside him.

After the ceremony, slaves will fill the pit with soil.

Kings and nobles

Around 1027BC, the Shang kings were conquered by people called the Zhou. The new Zhou kings allowed noble families to own land in return for their loyalty and help in times of war.

A Zhou noble in his war chariot

As the nobles became more powerful, the Zhou kings began to lose control. Nobles set up their own small kingdoms and fought each other constantly to try to win more land.

Confucius

A thinker called K'ung Fu-tzu (or Confucius) lived during this troubled time. He taught that war would only end when people knew the right way to behave. People should obey their rulers, and rulers should be kind to their people.

Confucius

Mastering metal

Craftworkers in Shang China learned how to make weapons and containers from bronze. People used elaborate bronze cauldrons to prepare food and wine for their dead ancestors, who they thought were gods.

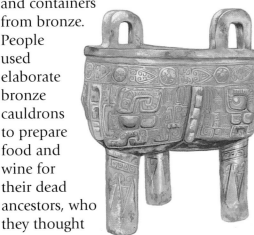

Bronze cauldron

Writing on bones

Writing in China began around 1400BC. To help them tell the future, priests carved questions on bones called oracle bones. They heated the bones until they cracked, and then "read" the pattern made by the cracks to find the answers to their questions.

Early Chinese writing

Oracle bone

THE FAR EAST

China's First Emperor

This picture shows part of the Great Wall of China.

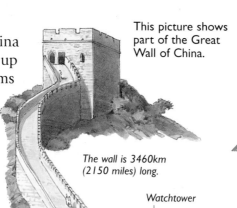

A Chinese noble

By around 480BC, China was made up of seven kingdoms which were constantly at war with each other. By 221BC, the kingdom of Qin (pronounced "chin") had conquered all the others, and the King of Qin controlled a huge empire. He called himself Qin Shi Huangdi, which means "First Emperor of China".

Qin Shi Huangdi

The wall is 3460km (2150 miles) long.

Watchtower

The Great Wall of China

Shi Huangdi had a massive wall built to protect his Empire from attacks by northern tribes (later called the Huns). The Great Wall was made by joining together a series of smaller walls put up by earlier rulers. It is still the biggest man-made structure in the world.

Controlling the nobles

To prevent powerful nobles from rebelling against him, Shi Huangdi forced them to move to the capital city, Xianyang, where he could keep an eye on them. Weapons belonging to the nobles' armies were taken away and melted down.

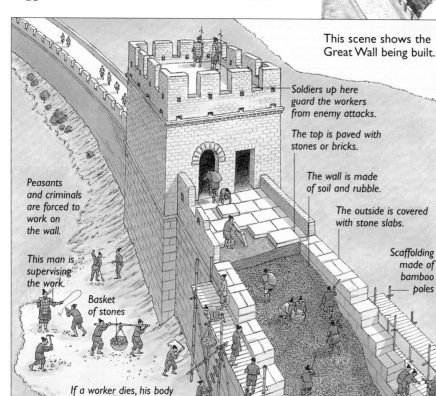

This scene shows the Great Wall being built.

Soldiers up here guard the workers from enemy attacks.

The top is paved with stones or bricks.

The wall is made of soil and rubble.

The outside is covered with stone slabs.

Scaffolding made of bamboo poles

Peasants and criminals are forced to work on the wall.

This man is supervising the work.

Basket of stones

If a worker dies, his body is built into the wall.

A low wall (or parapet) protects soldiers from enemy arrows.

If enemies attack, a fire is lit on top of the tower to warn other soldiers.

People travel along the wall.

Map of China

- ☐ Empire of Qin Shi Huangdi
- ᵞᵞᵞ The Great Wall

Yellow

Xianyang

YELLOW SEA

Yangtze

Punishing protestors

Shi Huangdi believed that people were evil and had to be forced to obey the law. Anyone who disobeyed was brutally punished. He ordered the burning of any books that did not agree with his ideas, and scholars who protested were thrown into a pit and buried alive.

This picture shows the burning of the books.

Scholars are thrown into a pit.

Uniting the Empire

Shi Huangdi built new roads and canals to link the different parts of his Empire. He also made everyone use the same type of coins and the same weights and measures. This made it much easier for people to trade with each other.

Chinese coins

To make sure that his orders could be understood by everyone, Shi Huangdi introduced a standard form of writing throughout the Empire.

This Chinese symbol means "by order of the emperor".

The terracotta army

When Shi Huangdi died in 210BC, he was buried in a huge tomb guarded by an army of over 7,500 life-size model warriors. The warriors were made of terracotta (a type of pottery) and carried real weapons. It is said that crossbows were set to fire automatically at anyone who tried to break into the tomb.

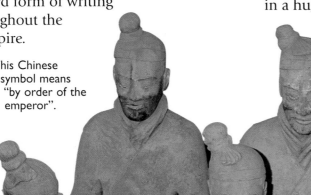

Terracotta warriors standing guard around the emperor's tomb

The face of each warrior is different.

2000BC   1000BC   500BC   AD1   AD500

The Han Dynasty

Wooden model of a Han noble

S oon after the first emperor died, rebellions broke out and the Empire collapsed. In 202BC, a soldier called Liu Bang took control of the country and made himself emperor. He was the first of a dynasty (family) of emperors called the Han, who ruled China for the next 400 years.

This scene shows part of Ch'ang-an, the capital city of the early Han emperors.

Official business

An official with his attendants

The Han emperors had lots of officials to help them run their Empire. The officials collected taxes, looked after roads and canals, and made sure that everyone obeyed the law.

Tough tests

Anyone who wanted to be an official had to take exams. People were asked questions on ancient poetry and the teachings of the thinker Confucius.

Officials taking an exam

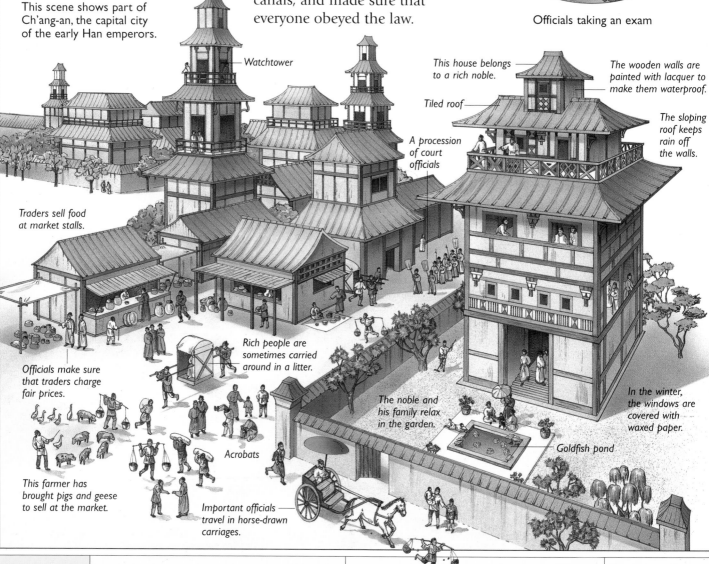

Watchtower

This house belongs to a rich noble.

The wooden walls are painted with lacquer to make them waterproof.

Tiled roof

The sloping roof keeps rain off the walls.

A procession of court officials

Traders sell food at market stalls.

Officials make sure that traders charge fair prices.

Rich people are sometimes carried around in a litter.

The noble and his family relax in the garden.

In the winter, the windows are covered with waxed paper.

Goldfish pond

Acrobats

This farmer has brought pigs and geese to sell at the market.

Important officials travel in horse-drawn carriages.

The Silk Road

Around 105BC, Chinese merchants began to travel across Asia to trade with merchants in the West.

Camels carried Chinese silk, spices and precious stones along a route known as the Silk Road, which stretched all the way from China to the Mediterranean Sea.

Chinese silk banner

Map of China

TO THE WEST

Ch'ang-an Yellow Luoyang

YELLOW SEA

Yangtze

SOUTH CHINA SEA

Han Empire
Silk Road

Tombs and treasure

Han tombs were filled with everything the dead person might need in the Next World, such as clothes, food, medicines, cups and bowls. One prince and his wife were buried in suits made of jade (a hard, green stone). People thought this would stop the bodies from rotting away.

Wooden bowl covered with shiny lacquer

Wars and quarrels

The Han emperors fought to defend the Empire against tribes of Huns from the north, and eventually defeated them. The Huns gave up attacking China and moved away to the west.

However, quarrels between the royal family and their courtiers weakened the power of the emperor. In AD220, the last Han emperor gave up his throne, and the Empire fell apart.

The jade burial suit of Princess Tou Wan

The suit is made from over 2,000 pieces of polished jade linked together with gold wire.

Inventions

The Chinese were the first people to make paper. They dipped a bamboo screen into a mixture of pulped tree bark, plants and rags. A thin layer of pulp was left to dry on the screen.

Chinese scientists invented many other things that are still used today, such as the compass, the wheelbarrow, and the ship's rudder (used for steering).

Making paper

Bamboo screen

Pulp

Chinese machine for detecting earthquakes

If the earth shakes, a ball falls into the toad's mouth, showing the direction of the earthquake.

Important dates

c.5000BC Farming begins in China.
c.4000BC Rice farming begins.
c.2700BC Silk making begins.
1766–1027BC The Shang dynasty
c.1400BC Writing on oracle bones
1027–221BC The Zhou dynasty
c.722–481BC The Zhou kings lose power. The nobles fight each other.
551BC Confucius is born.
481–221BC Seven kingdoms are at war (the Warring States Period).
221–210BC Qin Shi Huangdi rules as China's first emperor.
202BC–AD220 The Han dynasty
c.AD1–100 Buddhism spreads from India (see page 70).
c.AD100 Paper is invented.

THE FAR EAST

2000BC

500BC

AD1

AD500

The People of Ancient Japan

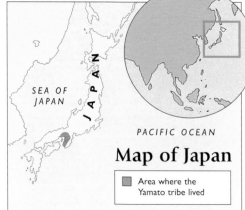

Map of Japan

SEA OF JAPAN

JAPAN

PACIFIC OCEAN

■ Area where the Yamato tribe lived

Jomon vase

From around 9000BC to 500BC, the people of Japan lived by hunting, fishing and collecting nuts and berries to eat. There was so much food around that they did not think of farming. This long period of time is called the Jomon Period.

Tombs and warriors

The early Yamato emperors were buried in stone tombs under enormous keyhole-shaped mounds of earth. Small clay models of warriors were placed around the mound to guard it.

This picture shows the tomb of a Yamato emperor.

This picture shows a typical Jomon village.

The thatched walls of the houses are held up by branches.

These hunters have caught a wild boar.

This man is trying to catch a tuna fish.

This girl is collecting shellfish.

This woman is coiling strips of clay to make a pot.

People wear animal skins.

This woman is cooking dinner.

Fishbones and old shells are thrown in a heap.

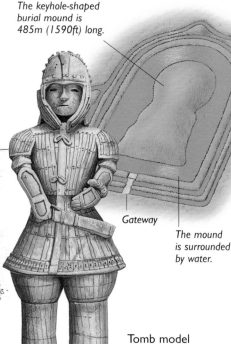

The keyhole-shaped burial mound is 485m (1590ft) long.

Gateway

The mound is surrounded by water.

Tomb model (or haniwa) of a Yamato warrior

Bronze bell

New skills

Around 500BC, settlers moved to Japan from the mainland of Asia. They brought new skills with them, such as rice farming and metalworking, and lived in tribes ruled by a chieftain.

The first emperors

A tribe called the Yamato gradually became more powerful than the others. The Yamato chieftains were the first emperors of Japan. During their rule, many new ideas, such as writing, were brought over from China.

The Japanese believed their emperors were descended from the Sun Goddess.

Important dates

c.9000-500BC	People hunt and fish for food (the Jomon Period).
c.500BC-AD300	Rice farming and metalworking begin (the Yayoi Period).
c.AD300-500	Yamato rulers take control of central Japan.
c.AD450	Writing is introduced from China.

JAPANESE

10,000BC   5000BC   4000BC   3000BC

The Riches of Arabia

The deserts of Arabia are among the hottest and driest places on earth. Only a few nomads (wandering people) lived there, roaming around from one water hole to another.

Arab nomads lived in tents.

Around 1000BC, Arabs learned how to tame camels, which meant they could travel farther across the desert.

Camels can travel for up to eight days without water.

Kingdoms of the south

Along the south coast of Arabia, where there was more rain, rich kingdoms grew up. The most famous is Sabaea. Its capital city, Ma'rib, had a huge dam to control the water supply.

The Bible tells how the Queen of Sabaea (or Sheba) visited King Solomon of Israel.

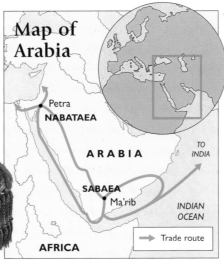

Map of Arabia

Petra
NABATAEA
ARABIA
TO INDIA
SABAEA
Ma'rib
INDIAN OCEAN
AFRICA

→ Trade route

Sweet smells

In the southern kingdoms, two special types of bushes grew. Their sap was used to make frankincense and myrrh (types of sweet-smelling incense).

Collecting sap to make incense

Incense was burned in religious ceremonies all over the ancient world as an offering to the gods. It was also used to make perfumes and medicines.

An Egyptian priest burning incense

Arab traders with their camels

Routes to riches

Merchants from India brought spices and jewels to ports on the south coast of Arabia. Arab traders carried these goods to Egypt or the Mediterranean, and sold them at a great price.

The city of Petra

At the northern end of the trade routes was the kingdom of Nabataea. Its capital city, Petra, was built in a narrow valley surrounded by rocky cliffs.

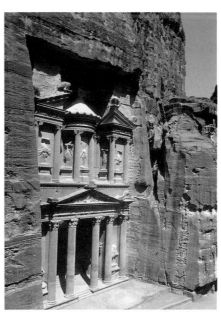

Rich people of Petra had spectacular tombs carved out of solid rock.

Important dates

c.1000BC	The Arabs tame camels.
c.500BC–AD100	Sabaea is at its most powerful.
c.100BC–AD150	Nabataea is rich and powerful.

THE MIDDLE EAST

ARABS

2000BC — 1000BC — 500BC — AD1 — AD500

Life in Ancient Africa

Kushite pots

Thousands of years ago, the Sahara Desert was an area of grassland and lakes. The people who lived there hunted wild cattle, giraffes, rhinos and hippos. Then, around 6000BC, the Saharan people learned how to tame animals and began to herd cattle rather than hunt them.

Saharan rock painting of herdsmen with their cattle

By 4000BC, dry weather had turned the grassland into desert. The Sahara Desert split Africa in two, and life north of the Sahara developed very differently from life in the south.

Map of Africa

- ■ Area where the Nok people lived
- → Route of the Bantu people

The kingdom of Kush

For hundreds of years, the kingdom of Kush in the Nile Valley was ruled by the Egyptians. Around 1000BC, the Kushites broke free and later went on to conquer Egypt themselves.

Egyptian picture of a Kushite prisoner of war

Until around 590BC, the capital city of Kush was at Napata. Then, a new capital was built at Meroë where there was better farmland. The people of Meroë mined iron, which they used to make weapons and tools. They grew rich by trading with India and the lands around the Mediterranean.

The kings and queens of Meroë were buried under steep-sided pyramids.

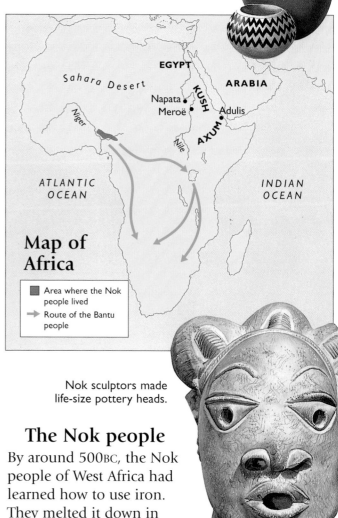

Nok sculptors made life-size pottery heads.

The Nok people

By around 500BC, the Nok people of West Africa had learned how to use iron. They melted it down in clay furnaces and shaped it into strong tools. These tools helped them to become successful farmers.

This picture shows Nok people using a furnace.

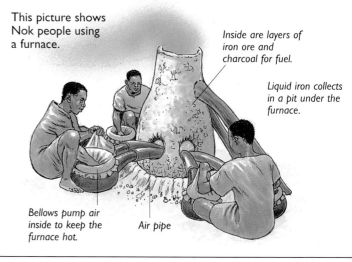

Inside are layers of iron ore and charcoal for fuel.

Liquid iron collects in a pit under the furnace.

Bellows pump air inside to keep the furnace hot.

Air pipe

10,000BC	5000BC		4000BC	3000BC

The spread of farming

Most Africans south of the Sahara hunted wild animals and gathered plants to eat, but the Bantu tribes of West Africa were farmers. Around 500BC, they began to move south and east looking for new land. By AD500, they had reached the southern tip of Africa, and farming had spread to most of the continent.

A cutaway picture of a Bantu house

The inside is plastered with clay.

This man is making farming tools from iron.

Framework of wooden poles

Layers of clay and thatched grass

The floor is raised on wooden logs.

Doorway

The riches of Axum

Around AD100, the kingdom of Axum grew up on the Red Sea coast. Axum became rich by trading with Arabia, India and parts of the Roman Empire. Merchants from other lands stopped at the port of Adulis on their way to and from India.

This scene shows merchants at the port of Adulis.

A ship loaded with spices from India

These monkeys will be taken abroad and sold as pets.

Frankincense and myrrh from Arabia

African slaves for sale

This Axumite merchant is selling African ivory, gold and emeralds.

Cloth from the Roman Empire

Jars of wine and oil from Rome

Standing stones

The kings of Axum used some of their wealth to build magnificent palaces and tall stone towers. Each tower marked the tomb of a king.

The huge tower shown here was carved from a single block of stone.

A Christian king

Around AD320, missionaries brought the Christian religion to Axum, and King Ezana of Axum became the first Christian king in Africa. (See pages 88 and 89 for more about Christianity.)

Axumite gold coin

The cross is used as a Christian symbol.

Important dates

c.6000BC	People in the Sahara tame cattle.
c.4000BC	The Sahara grasslands have turned to desert.
c.1600-1000BC	The kingdom of Kush is ruled by Egypt.
c.750-664BC	Kushite kings conquer and rule Egypt.
c.590BC	Meroë becomes the capital city of Kush.
c.500BC-AD200	The Nok people are at their most successful.
c.500BC-AD500	The Bantu people move through Africa.
c.AD100-700	The kingdom of Axum is rich and powerful.
c.AD330-350	King Ezana rules Axum.

AFRICA

2000BC	1000BC	500BC	AD1	AD500

The Ideas of India

Around 1500BC, tribes of people known as Aryans began to arrive in the Indus Valley (in modern Pakistan). Gradually, they spread out across northern India and settled down.

From hymns to Hinduism

Aryan priests sang hymns to their many gods. The Aryans did not write, so the hymns were passed on by word of mouth. Many years later, they were written down in holy books called the Vedas. These writings became very important in the Hindu religion, which is the main religion in India today.

Shiva the destroyer, one of the many Hindu gods

A class of their own

The early Aryans divided people into different classes according to their jobs. Later, children always belonged to the same class as their parents. This way of grouping people was known as the caste system.

Priests and scholars

Warriors and kings

Merchants and farmers

Workers

The four main groups in the caste system

The beginning of Buddhism

Siddhartha in his chariot

The Buddhist religion was started by an Indian prince called Siddhartha Gautama. One day, when he was out riding in his chariot, Siddhartha came across sickness, old age and death for the first time.

Siddhartha was very upset by what he saw and decided to find a way to escape suffering and live in peace. He left his palace and became a wandering holy man.

Siddhartha as a holy man

After many years, Siddhartha realized that people suffer because they want things and only care about themselves. Because of this understanding, he became known as the Buddha, which means the "enlightened one". People listened to the Buddha teaching, and his ideas spread.

Statue of the Buddha's head

Indian war elephants

Map of India

INDIA

• Sanchi

• Ajanta

ARABIAN SEA

BAY OF BENGAL

Indus

Ganges

☐ Mauryan Empire at its largest

The Mauryan Empire

By 500BC, northern India was made up of many small kingdoms. In 321BC, a warrior named Chandragupta Maurya seized one of these kingdoms and went on to conquer most of India, creating the Mauryan Empire. The Empire was at its largest under Chandragupta's grandson, Asoka.

A Buddhist emperor

For 11 years, Asoka fought to make his Empire bigger. Then, in one battle, so many people were killed that he decided to become a Buddhist and give up fighting. Asoka promised to rule his people with kindness, and had his promises carved on stone pillars all over his Empire.

These lions decorated the top of one of Asoka's pillars.

During Asoka's rule, many Buddhist monasteries and monuments were built. Huge stone domes, called stupas, were built at places connected with the Buddha's life.

The Great Stupa at Sanchi

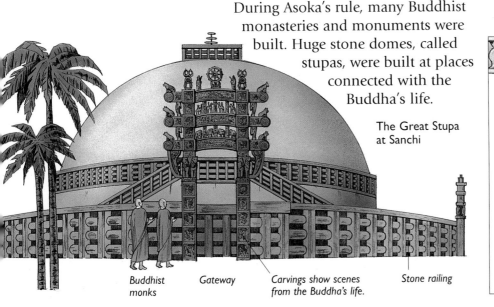

Buddhist monks

Gateway

Carvings show scenes from the Buddha's life.

Stone railing

Painting and poetry

After Asoka's death, the Empire grew weaker, and in the end it split up. India was not united again until AD320, when a new family of emperors called the Guptas took over.

The Gupta Empire is famous for its beautiful painting and sculpture. Classical Indian music and dance developed during this time, and the poet Kalidasa wrote about nature and love.

Part of a wall painting from the Buddhist cave temples at Ajanta

Important dates

c.1500BC The Aryans arrive.

c.560-480BC Siddhartha Gautama (the Buddha) lives.

327-325BC Alexander the Great tries to conquer north India (see pages 56 and 57).

321BC Chandragupta Maurya sets up the Mauryan Empire.

272-231BC Asoka is emperor.

185BC The Mauryan Empire collapses.

AD320-535 The Gupta Empire

SOUTH ASIA

2000BC   1000BC   500BC   AD1   AD500

The First North Americans

People first arrived in North America at least 15,000 years ago, and probably much earlier. At that time, a large part of the Earth was covered in ice and snow. America and Asia were joined by a bridge of land and ice, and the first North Americans walked across from Asia.

Hunting a mammoth

At first, people roamed around hunting large animals, such as mammoths, horses and buffalo, but by 8000BC most of these animals had died out. Hunters had to find smaller animals, and relied more on picking wild plants to eat.

Wild plants

Plums

Rosehips

A prickly pear

A gourd

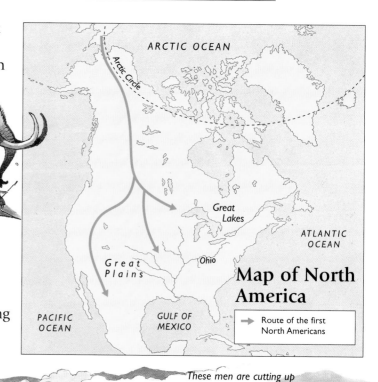

Map of North America

ARCTIC OCEAN

Arctic Circle

PACIFIC OCEAN

Great Plains

Great Lakes

Ohio

ATLANTIC OCEAN

GULF OF MEXICO

→ Route of the first North Americans

People spread out across the plains, woodlands, mountains, deserts and icy wastes of North America. They began to settle down, and a different way of life grew up in each of these areas.

These men are cutting up a dead buffalo.

This picture shows people of the Great Plains hunting buffalo.

This man has just thrown his spear.

Some buffalo are killed with spears.

The hunters are disguised as wolves.

The buffalo are being chased over the edge of a cliff.

Hunters of the Plains

Buffalo were one of the few large animals that did not die out, and the people of the Great Plains hunted them for their meat and skins. The skins were scraped clean and made into clothes and tents.

Scraping a buffalo skin

THE AMERICAS

10,000BC   5000BC   4000BC

72

Ivory knife used
for cutting ice

Hunters of the Arctic

The people who settled in the far north had to survive in the freezing lands of the Arctic. They caught fish, and hunted walrus and seals. In winter, they used blocks of ice to build shelters called igloos.

A cutaway picture of an igloo

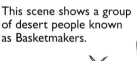

Clear ice window

Blocks of ice stuck together with snow

This tunnel stops cold air from getting inside.

Wooden sled

Woodland tribes

The Adena people lived in the eastern woodlands along the Ohio River. They hunted deer, caught fish and collected berries. They also grew plants, such as beans, gourds and sunflowers.

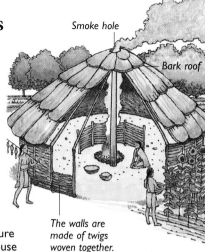

Smoke hole

Bark roof

A cutaway picture of an Adena house

The walls are made of twigs woven together.

The Adena, and the Hopewell people who came after them, are famous for the huge earth mounds they built. Some of the mounds were pyramid-shaped, but others were shaped like animals.

The Great Serpent Mound is 217m (712ft) long.

Desert tribes

In the deserts of the southwest, people lived by hunting small animals and collecting nuts, seeds and wild fruits. Later, some tribes learned to grow corn, beans and squashes.

This scene shows a group of desert people known as Basketmakers.

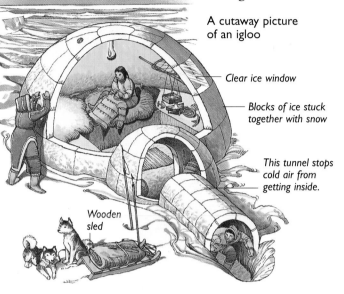

This boy is picking fruit from a cactus plant.

Baskets for carrying water are lined with gum from plants.

Babies are carried in backpacks called cradleboards.

This woman is weaving a basket from twigs.

The houses are built partly underground.

These men have caught some rabbits.

The Hopewell traded with other tribes from the Great Lakes to the Gulf of Mexico. They brought back copper, shells and alligator teeth, which they used to make necklaces and ornaments.

Carved copper bird

Important dates

c.10,000–8000BC	Early North Americans hunt large animals.
c.8000–1000BC	People spread out and learn new ways of life.
c.2000BC	People settle in the Arctic.
c.1000–300BC	The Adena people
c.300BC–AD550	The Hopewell people
c.AD1–500	Early Basketmakers

The People of Ancient Peru

Squash

Pepper

Potatoes

South American vegetables

Chili peppers

By 2000BC, the people of ancient Peru had settled down to farm, and were growing corn, peppers, chili peppers, squashes and potatoes. Farmers kept llamas for their meat, milk and wool, and also used them for carrying loads.

Llama

Map of Peru

PACIFIC OCEAN

P E R U

•Paracas

— Chavín homeland
◻ Moche homeland
◻ Nazca homeland

Drawings in the desert

The Nazca people are famous for the giant outlines of animals and shapes that they made in the desert. Experts think that these drawings may have been done to persuade the gods to send rain.

The giant spider shown in this picture is 45m (148ft) long.

Gods and gold

Around 1200BC, the Chavín people created the first civilization in South America. They were skilled stoneworkers and built huge temples filled with sculptures and carvings of their snarling, animal-like gods. The Chavín were also the first people in the Americas to make things from gold.

This gold ornament may have been made for a Chavín priest.

Cloth pictures

Paracas embroidery

The Paracas people of southern Peru were skilled at weaving and embroidery. When someone died, the body was placed in a basket and was wrapped in layers of beautifully embroidered cloth.

Priests and pottery

In the north, the Moche people were ruled by powerful warrior-priests. They conquered nearby tribes, and often sacrificed prisoners of war to their gods. The Moche are famous for making pots in human shapes.

A pot in the shape of a Moche warrior

Important dates

C.2000BC	The people of Peru first grow corn.
C.1200-300BC	The Chavín people
C.500BC-AD200	The Paracas people
C.200BC-AD600	The Nazca people
C.AD1-700	The Moche people

10,000BC	5000BC	4000BC	3000BC

Corn plant

The Olmecs

The Olmecs lived on a swampy plain beside the Gulf of Mexico. They had no farm animals to provide them with meat, so growing crops was very important. Corn was the main crop, but farmers also grew beans, squashes, chili peppers and avocados.

Map of Olmec lands

GULF OF MEXICO

• La Venta

San Lorenzo •

PACIFIC OCEAN

▪ Area where the Olmecs lived

Gods and games

By around 1200BC, the Olmecs had begun building a series of temples to their gods at a place called San Lorenzo. Later, San Lorenzo was destroyed and a new place of worship was built at La Venta.

Carving of the Olmecs' jaguar god

This picture shows a religious ceremony at La Venta.

Some experts think this mosaic shows the face of the jaguar god.

The mosaic has just been finished.

Priest

Blocks of green stone

Blue clay

The mosaic is buried immediately, because it is too holy to look at.

As part of their religion, the Olmecs played a sacred ball game. Players used a hard rubber ball and wore helmets to protect their heads. Some of the players may have been sacrificed at the end of the game.

Olmec ball-players

Huge heads

The Olmecs are best known for the massive stone heads that they carved. Some of these are almost 3m (10ft) high. Experts think that the heads may show different Olmec rulers.

This huge stone head was carved from a single block of stone.

The end of the Olmecs

Around 400BC, the temples at La Venta were abandoned. The Olmecs died out, but their way of life influenced many of the people who came after them (see pages 76 and 77).

Important dates

c.1200BC San Lorenzo is built.
c.900BC San Lorenzo is destroyed.
c.400BC La Venta is abandoned.

THE AMERICAS

SOUTH AMERICA

CENTRAL AMERICA

2000BC   1000BC   500BC   AD1   AD500

Ancient Cities of the Americas

The city of Teotihuacán (in modern Mexico) was the biggest ancient city in the Americas. People began building it around 100BC, and by AD500 it was the sixth largest city in the world.

In the middle of Teotihuacán was the Citadel, where the rulers of the city lived in splendid palaces. Most other people lived in large apartment buildings, which had room for several families.

The rain god of Teotihuacán

Crafts

Craftworkers in Teotihuacán shaped pots and figures from clay, carved ornaments from polished stones and shells, and made tools and weapons from obsidian (a hard glassy rock).

Clay figure from Teotihuacán

Trade

Teotihuacán was an important trading city. In the marketplace, merchants traded pottery and obsidian tools for seashells, sweet-smelling incense and the beautiful tail feathers of the quetzal bird. The feathers were used to decorate the clothes of rich people.

Quetzal bird

This picture shows part of the city of Teotihuacán.

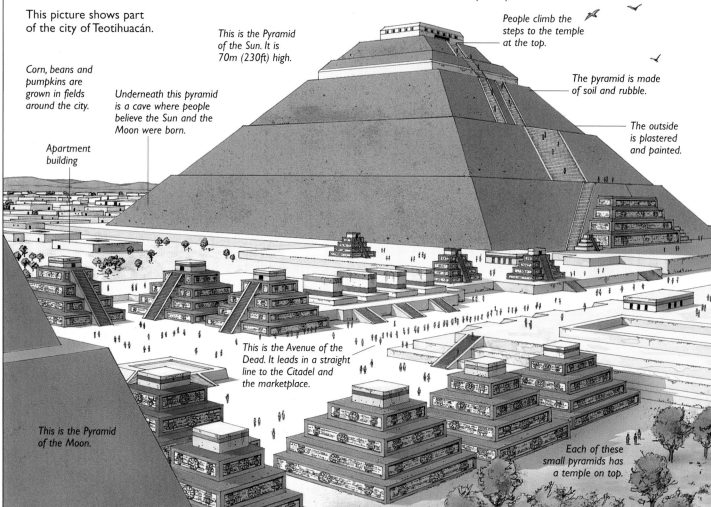

Corn, beans and pumpkins are grown in fields around the city.

Underneath this pyramid is a cave where people believe the Sun and the Moon were born.

Apartment building

This is the Pyramid of the Sun. It is 70m (230ft) high.

People from all over Central America come to worship at the city's temples.

People climb the steps to the temple at the top.

The pyramid is made of soil and rubble.

The outside is plastered and painted.

This is the Pyramid of the Moon.

This is the Avenue of the Dead. It leads in a straight line to the Citadel and the marketplace.

Each of these small pyramids has a temple on top.

THE AMERICAS

These men are carving a giant stone pillar.

Cities in the jungle

The spectacular stone cities of the Maya people lay deep in the Central American rainforest. Mayan cities were built around a complex of squares, temples, palaces and ball courts (where people played a sacred ball game). The buildings were covered in carvings of Mayan gods and kings.

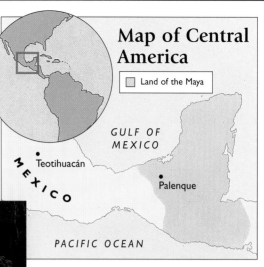

Map of Central America

☐ Land of the Maya

GULF OF MEXICO

MEXICO

• Teotihuacán

• Palenque

PACIFIC OCEAN

The Temple of Inscriptions in the city of Palenque

Words and numbers

The Maya invented a writing system using picture signs (or glyphs) and wrote in

Part of a Mayan book

books made of bark paper. Experts are just beginning to understand what this writing means.

Zero   One   Five

The Maya used three symbols to write all the numbers. They were using the number "zero" hundreds of years before anyone else thought of the idea.

Twelve

Blood, war and sacrifice

The Maya had many gods, and thought they could please them by making offerings of human blood. One way of doing this was to pull a string of thorns through a hole in the tongue.

Carving of a queen offering blood

The kings of the different Mayan cities were often at war with each other. They fought for power and riches, and took prisoners to sacrifice to their gods.

Feather headdress

Jaguar skin

Mayan warrior

Important dates

c.300BC   The Maya begin building stone cities.

c.100BC-AD250   Teotihuacán is built.

c.AD250-900   The Maya are at their most successful.

c.AD500   Teotihuacán is rich and powerful.

c.AD750   Teotihuacán is destroyed in a fire.

THE AMERICAS

2000BC   1000BC   500BC   AD1   AD500

77

The Celtic Tribes

The people known as Celts were made up of many different tribes, but they all had a similar language and way of life. This way of life had grown up near a place called Hallstatt (in modern Austria) by around 800BC.

The Celts gradually spread out across most of Europe, settling in the lands they conquered. One group even settled as far away as Asia Minor (modern Turkey).

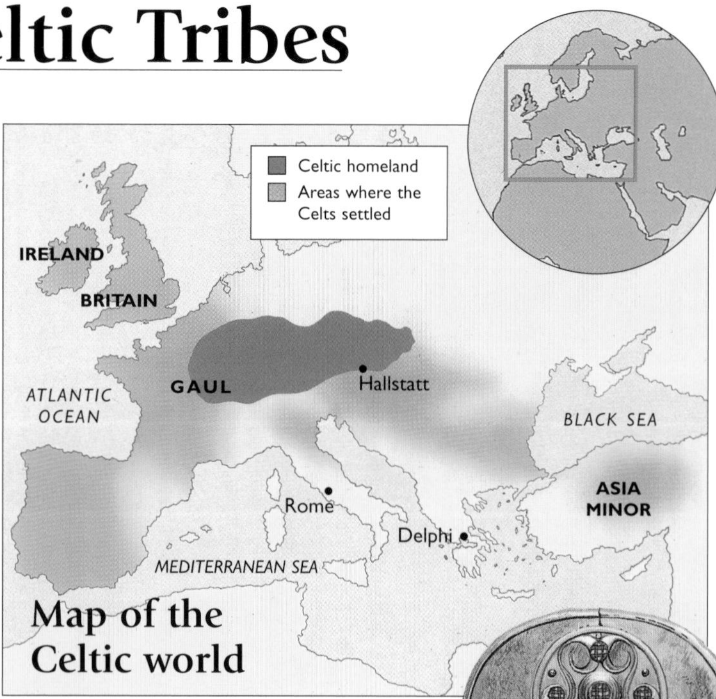

Celtic statue of a boar, a symbol of strength

Map of the Celtic world

- Celtic homeland
- Areas where the Celts settled

IRELAND
BRITAIN
ATLANTIC OCEAN
GAUL
Hallstatt
Rome
Delphi
MEDITERRANEAN SEA
BLACK SEA
ASIA MINOR

Life at home

Wherever the Celts settled, they set up farms and small villages. Their houses were built of wood or stone and had one big room inside, where the family cooked, ate and slept.

This cutaway picture shows a typical Celtic house.

Celtic crafts

The Celts were highly skilled metalworkers. They used iron to make strong weapons and tools, and created beautiful objects from bronze, silver and gold.

A gold neckband, called a torc

This bronze shield was found in the Thames in London.

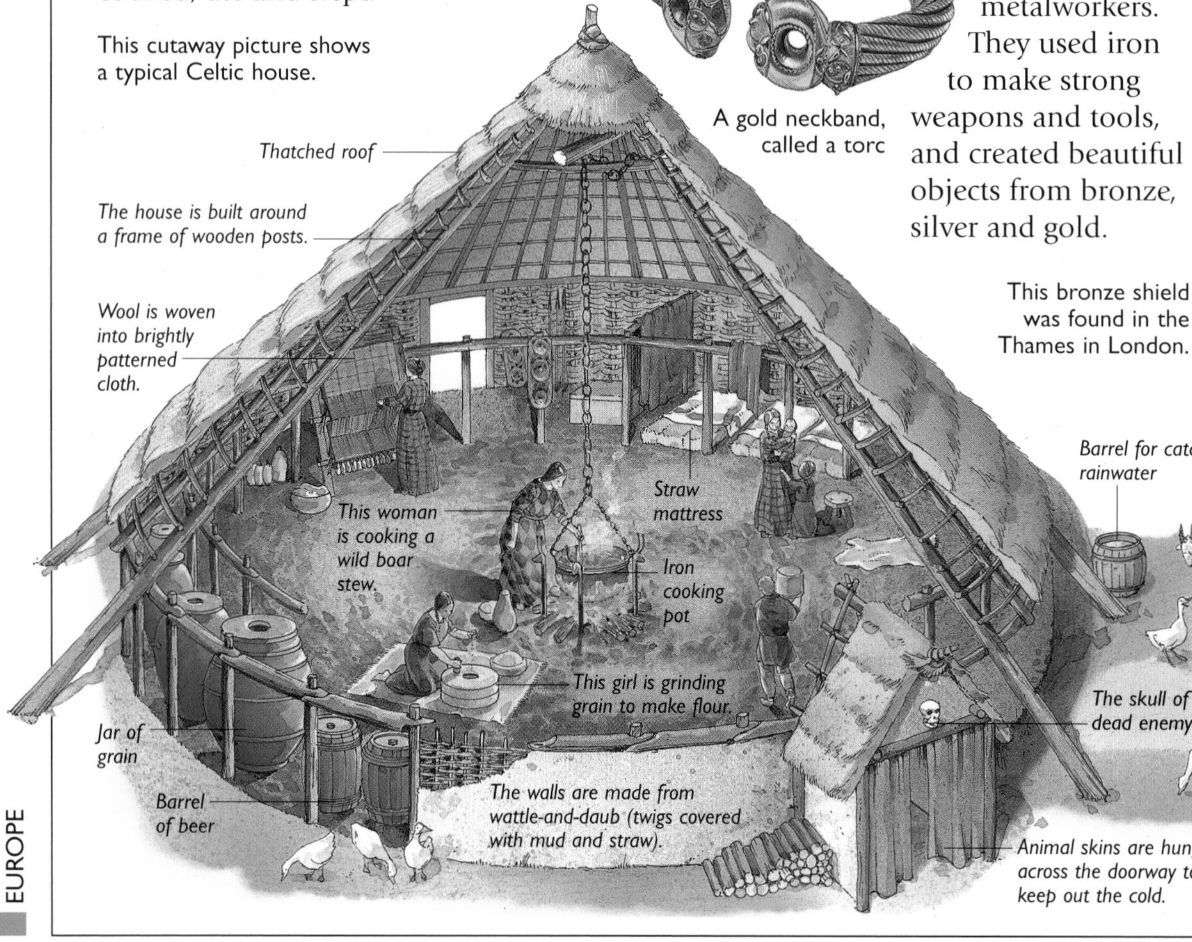

Thatched roof

The house is built around a frame of wooden posts.

Wool is woven into brightly patterned cloth.

This woman is cooking a wild boar stew.

Straw mattress

Iron cooking pot

This girl is grinding grain to make flour.

Jar of grain

Barrel of beer

The walls are made from wattle-and-daub (twigs covered with mud and straw).

Barrel for catching rainwater

This man is chopping wood for the fire.

The skull of a dead enemy

Animal skins are hung across the doorway to keep out the cold.

These boys are playing with dice.

Forts and fighting

The Celts were fierce warriors and their tribes often fought each other. They built large hilltop forts to protect their women, children and animals from attacks by enemies.

The hillfort is surrounded by huge mounds of earth with ditches in between.

Houses

This picture shows Celtic warriors charging at an enemy.

Nobles ride chariots into battle and then fight on foot.

War trumpets make a terrifying noise.

Warriors comb lime through their hair to make it spiky.

Wooden shield covered with leather

Some warriors fight on horseback.

Chariot wheels have a strong iron rim.

Warriors run yelling at the enemy.

Some warriors paint blue patterns on their bodies to make themselves look scary.

Feasts

Warriors held great feasts to celebrate their victories in battle. They were entertained by poet-musicians, called bards, who recited poems about the brave deeds of Celtic heroes.

A Celtic feast

A bard chanting a poem

Harp

This is the chieftain (leader) of the tribe.

Flagon of wine

A pig roasting on a spit

Religion

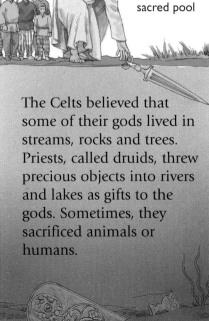

A druid dropping a sword into a sacred pool

The Celts believed that some of their gods lived in streams, rocks and trees. Priests, called druids, threw precious objects into rivers and lakes as gifts to the gods. Sometimes, they sacrificed animals or humans.

Roman conquerors

As the Roman Empire grew, the Celts fought hard to defend their lands. However, they were no match for the mighty Roman army, and in the end most of them were conquered. The Celtic way of life only survived in Ireland and in remote parts of Scotland and Wales.

Important dates

c.800BC The Celtic way of life first appears.

c.390BC The Celts destroy part of Rome.

c.279BC The Celts attack and rob the Greek temple at Delphi.

c.278BC The Celts reach Asia Minor.

58-51BC The Roman general Julius Caesar conquers the Celts in Gaul (modern France).

AD43 The Romans invade Britain.

EUROPE

| 2000BC | | 1000BC | 500BC | AD1 | AD500 |

79

The Rise of Rome

The city of Rome began as a small farming village by a river called the Tiber. As time passed, more villages were built and eventually they joined together to form a city.

An early village in the Tiber Valley

The story of Romulus

According to a Roman legend, the city was set up by a man named Romulus. As babies, he and his twin brother Remus had been left to die near the Tiber. They were found by a wolf, who fed them until they were rescued by a shepherd.

Statue of the wolf feeding Romulus and Remus

When the twins grew up, they decided to build a city on the banks of the Tiber, but they had a violent quarrel. Romulus killed his brother and named the city after himself. Tradition says this happened in 753BC.

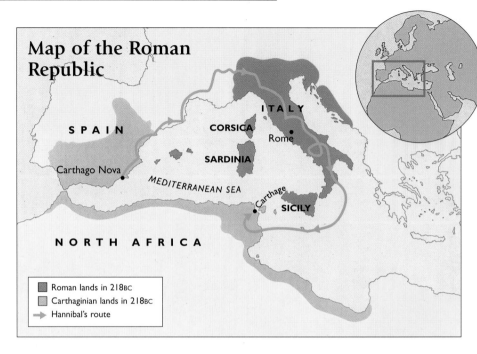

Map of the Roman Republic

SPAIN

ITALY

CORSICA

Rome

SARDINIA

Carthago Nova

MEDITERRANEAN SEA

Carthage

SICILY

NORTH AFRICA

- ◼ Roman lands in 218BC
- ◼ Carthaginian lands in 218BC
- ➔ Hannibal's route

The Roman Republic

Until around 509BC, Rome was ruled by kings. Then, the last king was driven out of the city and Rome became a republic. The Roman Republic was ruled by the Senate, a group of men (called senators) who came from the city's most important families. Led by the Senate, the Romans gradually conquered all of Italy.

Coin showing the Senate House

This picture shows a meeting of the Senate. (Part of the seating has been cut away.)

Senators wear a toga (robe) with a purple stripe.

Each year, some senators are chosen by the people to do special jobs.

This senator organizes entertainment, such as chariot races. He is very popular.

This senator is a judge. He is making a speech about a new law.

Guard

These two men are in charge of the Senate this year. They are called consuls.

EUROPE

| 10,000BC | 5000BC | | 4000BC | | 3000BC |

80

Conquering Carthage

In 264BC, a series of wars broke out between the Romans and the people of Carthage in North Africa. Both sides fought fiercely over who should control trade around the Mediterranean Sea.

The Carthaginians invaded Italy in 218BC. This picture shows them crossing the Alps.

The Carthaginian general, Hannibal, leading his troops

Only two of the 40 war elephants survived the journey.

10,000 soldiers died in the mountains.

The wars between Rome and Carthage are known as the Punic Wars. They ended in 146BC when Carthage was completely destroyed. The Romans took over the Carthaginian lands and went on to conquer all the kingdoms around the Mediterranean.

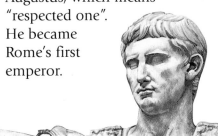

The city of Carthage in flames

Julius Caesar

As the Romans won more land, the senators argued over how things should be run. Rival groups of senators used the army to help them fight for power. In 49BC, a general called Julius Caesar marched with his army to Rome and seized power. Caesar brought peace, but some senators grew worried that he planned to make himself king, so they stabbed him to death.

Julius Caesar

The first emperor

After Julius Caesar died, there were more struggles for power. In 31BC, Caesar's great-nephew, Octavian, defeated his rival, Mark Antony, and won control of Rome. Octavian took the name Augustus, which means "respected one". He became Rome's first emperor.

Statue of the Emperor Augustus

Augustus is shown wearing the uniform of a Roman general.

2000BC	1000BC	500BC	AD1	AD500

The Roman Army

By the time Augustus became emperor, Rome controlled most of the land around the Mediterranean Sea. Over the next 150 years, the Romans conquered even more land, creating a vast empire that stretched from Britain to the Middle East. The Empire was at its largest in AD117 during the rule of the Emperor Trajan.

Emperor Augustus

Emperor Trajan

The Romans won wars because they had a strong, well-organized army, and their soldiers fought in highly disciplined groups. A group of 80 soldiers was called a century, centuries were grouped into cohorts, and ten cohorts made up a legion.

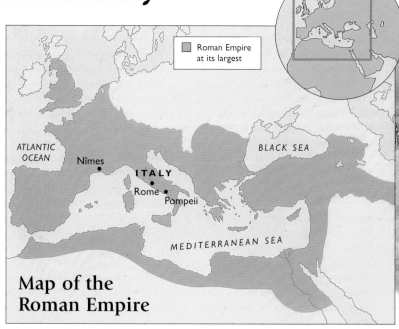

Roman Empire at its largest

ATLANTIC OCEAN

BLACK SEA

Nîmes

ITALY

Rome

Pompeii

MEDITERRANEAN SEA

Map of the Roman Empire

A Roman legionary (foot soldier)

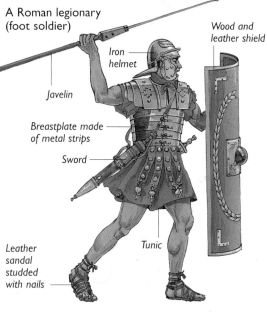

Iron helmet

Javelin

Wood and leather shield

Breastplate made of metal strips

Sword

Tunic

Leather sandal studded with nails

During the Republic, any man who owned land could be asked to fight for a while. By the time of the emperors, most soldiers were well-trained professionals, who made the army their career.

Attacking a city

The Romans were determined fighters and even conquered cities that were very well defended. They surrounded a city so no one could escape, and then used clever techniques to force their way in.

This scene shows the Roman army attacking a walled city.

Soldiers move around under a roof of shields. This is called a tortoise.

Soldiers have built a ramp over uneven ground.

A wooden siege tower is wheeled into position.

The tower is covered with strong metal plates.

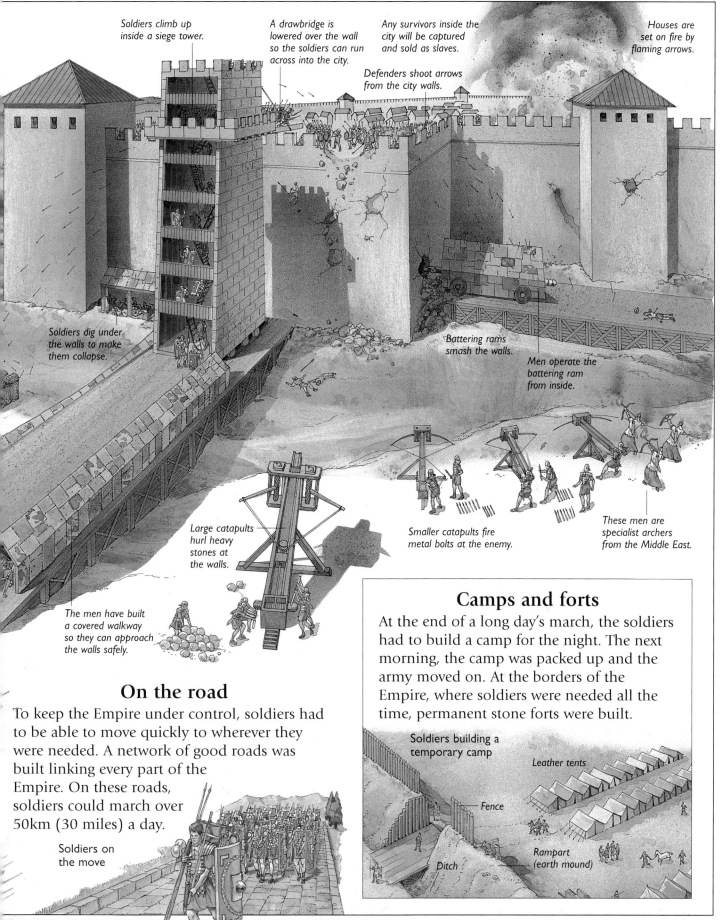

Soldiers climb up inside a siege tower.

A drawbridge is lowered over the wall so the soldiers can run across into the city.

Any survivors inside the city will be captured and sold as slaves.

Houses are set on fire by flaming arrows.

Defenders shoot arrows from the city walls.

Soldiers dig under the walls to make them collapse.

Battering rams smash the walls.

Men operate the battering ram from inside.

The men have built a covered walkway so they can approach the walls safely.

Large catapults hurl heavy stones at the walls.

Smaller catapults fire metal bolts at the enemy.

These men are specialist archers from the Middle East.

On the road

To keep the Empire under control, soldiers had to be able to move quickly to wherever they were needed. A network of good roads was built linking every part of the Empire. On these roads, soldiers could march over 50km (30 miles) a day.

Soldiers on the move

Camps and forts

At the end of a long day's march, the soldiers had to build a camp for the night. The next morning, the camp was packed up and the army moved on. At the borders of the Empire, where soldiers were needed all the time, permanent stone forts were built.

Soldiers building a temporary camp

Leather tents

Fence

Ditch

Rampart (earth mound)

2000BC   1000BC   500BC   AD1   AD500

Life in a Roman Town

The Romans took their way of life to all the lands they conquered. Each area, or province, of the Empire was run by a governor who made sure that people paid their taxes, obeyed Roman laws and respected Roman gods.

Statue of Jupiter, king of the gods

Retired Roman soldiers settled down to farm the land they had conquered, settlements grew up near Roman camps and forts, and new towns were built all over the Empire.

Roman towns were very well planned. They had many fine public buildings, such as temples and baths, as well as houses, apartment blocks, shops and restaurants.

This scene shows a busy Roman town. Some of the walls have been cut away to let you see inside the buildings.

Temple

Public bathhouse where people wash, swim and relax

The top floors are made of wood and often catch fire.

Firefighters use buckets of water to put out the fire.

Tiled roof

Most people live in large apartment blocks, called insulae.

Poorer families live in small rooms at the top.

Toilets are connected to underground drains.

Graffiti

School

Richer people have large, comfortable rooms.

There are shops at street level.

People get water from the fountain.

Bakery

Butcher's shop

Stepping stones for crossing the street

EUROPE

10,000BC   5000BC   3000BC

84

A life of luxury

While most townspeople lived in crowded apartment blocks, rich people had spacious houses with shady gardens. The houses were beautifully decorated inside. Some even had central heating under the floors and their own water supply.

This picture shows the reception hall (or atrium) of a Roman house.

This huge aqueduct, near the French town of Nîmes, is 49m (160ft) high.

Mosaic floor made of tiny pieces of stone

Rainwater collects in a pool.

Waterworks

Roman towns needed lots of fresh water to supply public baths, fountains and toilets. A system of pipes and channels (called aqueducts) took water to where it was needed. Engineers built tunnels and bridges to carry the water pipes across hills and valleys.

Buried treasure

Pompeii in southern Italy was a large, wealthy town. In August AD79, the nearby volcano Mount Vesuvius erupted. Pompeii was buried under clouds of ash and rivers of scorching lava (liquid rock). Experts have since dug through the lava to uncover the town, giving us an amazing picture of everyday life in Roman times.

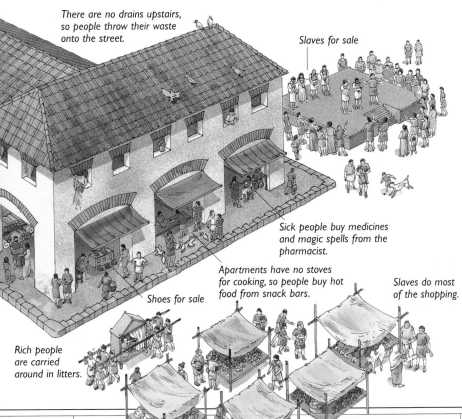

There are no drains upstairs, so people throw their waste onto the street.

Slaves for sale

Sick people buy medicines and magic spells from the pharmacist.

Apartments have no stoves for cooking, so people buy hot food from snack bars.

Slaves do most of the shopping.

Shoes for sale

Rich people are carried around in litters.

Wall painting at Pompeii

Fun and Games

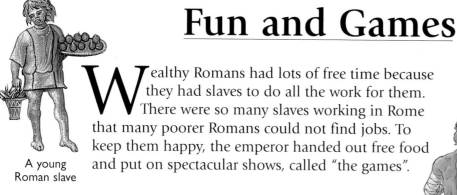

A young Roman slave

Wealthy Romans had lots of free time because they had slaves to do all the work for them. There were so many slaves working in Rome that many poorer Romans could not find jobs. To keep them happy, the emperor handed out free food and put on spectacular shows, called "the games".

Trident

This net is used by the gladiator to tangle his opponent.

This picture shows two types of gladiators.

This gladiator carries a net and trident.

This gladiator is more heavily armed.

Gladiator shows

Most gladiators were slaves or criminals, who were made to fight to entertain the crowds. At the end of a fight, the spectators decided if the loser should live or die. Thousands of gladiators were killed in this brutal sport.

Fights took place in huge stone stadiums, called amphitheatres. The biggest of these was the Colosseum in Rome, which held 50,000 people. Sometimes, the arena was flooded, so that gladiators could take part in sea battles.

This cutaway picture shows a sea battle in the Colosseum.

A huge awning can be hung from these poles to give shade for the spectators.

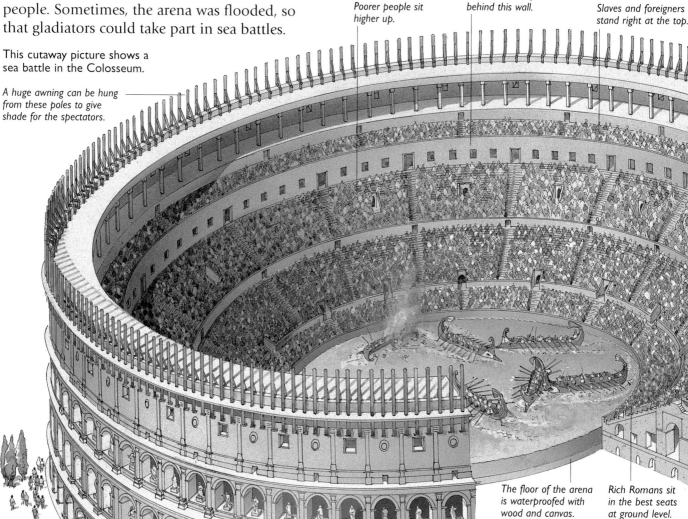

Poorer people sit higher up.

Women watch from behind this wall.

Slaves and foreigners stand right at the top.

The floor of the arena is waterproofed with wood and canvas.

Rich Romans sit in the best seats at ground level.

Chariot races

A driver and horses in a chariot race

The reins are wound around the driver's body.

Racing chariots are very light for extra speed.

The most popular of the games were the chariot races, which were held at a racetrack called a circus. The races were exciting to watch but were very dangerous, as drivers were often thrown off and killed.

There are four teams. Drivers wear red, blue, green or white to show which team they belong to.

Pastimes

As well as going to the games, Romans enjoyed relaxing in the public parks and gardens. They played board games and also liked gambling games.

Board game

Coins and dice for gambling

Children had seesaws, swings, kites, hoops, marbles and dolls to play with.

Sometimes, they rode around in small carts pulled by geese.

Wooden dolls

Mosaic showing a child in a toy cart

Drama

The first Roman plays were copied from Greek ones and were quite serious. By the time of the emperors, people preferred watching comedies. The shows gradually became more and more spectacular, with lots of music, dancing and special effects. Some actors became so popular that they were mobbed by their fans.

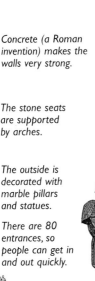

Concrete (a Roman invention) makes the walls very strong.

The stone seats are supported by arches.

The outside is decorated with marble pillars and statues.

There are 80 entrances, so people can get in and out quickly.

Roman actors in their costumes

Important dates

753BC The city of Rome is set up, according to legend.

c.509BC Rome becomes a republic.

246BC The Punic Wars start.

146BC The Romans destroy Carthage.

49BC Julius Caesar takes control of Rome.

27BC Augustus becomes the first Emperor of Rome.

AD72-80 The Colosseum is built.

AD117 The Roman Empire is at its largest.

EUROPE

| 2000BC | 1000BC | 500BC | AD1 | AD500 |

The Spread of Christianity

The Christian religion began with a Jew called Jesus, later known as Jesus Christ. You can read about his life and teachings in the New Testament of the Bible.

Mosaic showing Jesus as a shepherd

The life of Jesus

Jesus was born in Judea, a small province in the Roman Empire. At around the age of 30, he chose 12 men to be his disciples (followers) and began preaching. News spread that he could perform miracles, and crowds of people came to hear him.

This mosaic shows Jesus bringing a dead man back to life.

Jesus's teachings

Jesus taught that it was more important to love God and serve others than to obey the Jewish law. He said that people should stop doing wrong and make a fresh start, so that they could be part of God's kingdom.

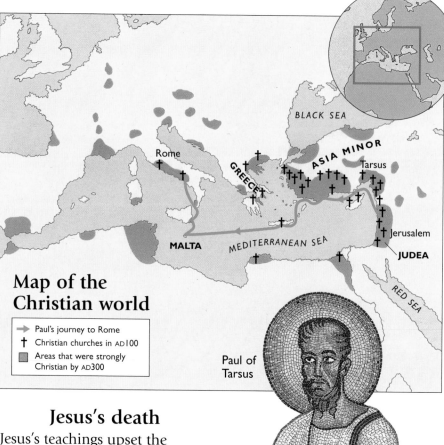

Map of the Christian world

→ Paul's journey to Rome
† Christian churches in AD100
▮ Areas that were strongly Christian by AD300

Paul of Tarsus

Jesus's death

Jesus's teachings upset the Jewish religious leaders, and the Romans were afraid that his ideas might lead to a rebellion in Judea. He was arrested in Jerusalem and was crucified (nailed to a cross to die).

Ivory carving of Jesus on the cross

Spreading the word

After Jesus died, his teachings were spread by his followers, who said that he had risen from the dead. Paul of Tarsus took the Christian message to Asia Minor (modern Turkey), to Greece and even to Rome.

On his way to Rome, Paul was shipwrecked off the coast of Malta.

10,000BC   5000BC   4000BC   3000BC

Hard times

Christianity spread quickly around the Roman Empire. Some emperors saw the Christians as rebels because they refused to worship Roman gods, and thousands were arrested, tortured and killed.

Many Christians were thrown to the lions for public entertainment.

To avoid being arrested, Christians often had to meet in secret. In Rome, they met in the catacombs, a series of tunnels under the city that were used as burial places.

This scene shows a group of Christians in the catacombs.

Secret symbols

Christians used secret signs to show other Christians that they shared the same faith. One of these was the Chi-Ro sign ✳.

Portrait of a Christian family with the Chi-Ro sign

The Chi-Ro sign was made up of the first two letters of the word "Christ" in Greek. It has been found carved on tombs, statues and doorways, and on the walls of the catacombs.

The ashes of dead people are stored in clay jars.

There are over 900km (560 miles) of tunnels.

The walls are painted with scenes from the Bible.

Christians meet to pray and to worship God.

Christian emperors

The Emperor Constantine was the first Roman ruler to accept the Christian faith. After seeing a cross of light in the sky, he sent his army into battle with the Chi-Ro sign on their shields. Constantine won the battle and later became a Christian.

Constantine riding into battle

Constantine gave Christians the freedom to worship openly, and helped to spread Christianity across Europe. He built the first great Christian churches, and gave Christians special privileges. Finally, in AD391, the Emperor Theodosius made Christianity the official religion of the Roman Empire.

Important dates

c.5BC Jesus Christ is born.

c.AD29 Jesus Christ is crucified.

AD45-58 Paul travels around Asia Minor and Greece.

AD58-60 Paul travels to Rome.

AD312 The Emperor Constantine makes Christianity legal.

AD391 Christianity becomes the official religion of the Roman Empire.

THE MIDDLE EAST

2000BC   1000BC   500BC   AD1   AD500

The Fall of Rome

Around AD200, the power of the Roman Empire began to weaken. The Roman armies started to choose their own emperors, and fighting broke out between different groups of soldiers. At the same time, the Empire was attacked by tribes from the northeast, known as Germani. The Romans called these people "barbarians".

A Germanic warrior

A throwing-axe, called a francisca

Map of the barbarian invasions

☐ Western Roman Empire	➡ Burgundians
☐ Eastern Roman Empire	➡ Alemanni
➡ Angles, Saxons, Jutes	➡ Lombards
➡ Franks	➡ Visigoths
➡ Vandals	➡ Ostrogoths

ATLANTIC OCEAN

BLACK SEA

Constantinople

Rome

MEDITERRANEAN SEA

Defending the Empire

In AD284, a general called Diocletian became emperor. To defend the Empire against the barbarians, he reorganized the army and made it bigger. Diocletian realized that the Empire was too big for one person to control, so he split it in two. He ruled the eastern half himself, while the western half was ruled by a general called Maximian. Each emperor had a deputy to help him rule.

Statue of Diocletian and Maximian with their two deputies

The Emperor Constantine

When Diocletian retired, there were more struggles for power. In AD312, Constantine became Emperor of the West. Later, he took control of the East as well, reuniting the Empire.

Constantine moved the capital of the Roman Empire to the town of Byzantium on the Black Sea. He rebuilt Byzantium, filled it with treasures from around the Empire and renamed it Constantinople, after himself.

A later mosaic of Constantine holding a model of Constantinople

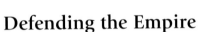

Asian invaders

Lasso

Hun warriors in battle

Around AD370, eastern Europe was invaded by people from central Asia, known as the Huns. As the Huns moved across Europe, they pushed the Germanic tribes off their land and into the Roman Empire.

Peace at a price

The Romans allowed some Germanic tribes, such as the Visigoths, to settle inside the Empire, as long as they helped to fight off other barbarians.

Visigoth settlers

Rome in ruins

In AD395, the Roman Empire split permanently into East and West, and from then on waves of barbarians swept across the Western Empire (see map). The city of Rome was attacked by the Visigoths in AD410, and by the Vandals in AD455.

This scene shows Vandal warriors wrecking Rome.

Many Romans are killed.

The end of the Empire

In AD476, a Visigoth chief called Odoacer made himself King of Italy, and the Western Empire came to an end. The Eastern Empire, with its capital at Constantinople, lasted for another thousand years.

Buildings are set on fire.

Statues are smashed.

Treasures are stolen.

Important dates

AD286	Diocletian splits the Roman Empire in two.
AD312	Constantine becomes Emperor of the West.
AD324	Constantine reunites the Empire.
C.AD370	The Huns arrive in Europe.
AD395	The Roman Empire splits permanently in two.
AD410	Rome is attacked by the Visigoths.
AD455	Rome is destroyed by the Vandals.
AD476	The Western Empire ends.

EUROPE

500BC   AD1   AD500

World Time Chart

This chart shows what was happening at the same time in different parts of the world.

DATE	THE AMERICAS	EUROPE	AFRICA
BEFORE 10,000BC	By c.13,000BC People arrive in North America.		
10,000BC	c.6000BC Farming begins in Central America.	c.6000BC Farming begins in Greece and spreads across Europe.	c.6000BC People in the Sahara tame cattle.

Saharan rock painting

DATE	THE AMERICAS	EUROPE	AFRICA
5000BC		c.3000-1500BC Stonehenge is built in Britain.	c.5000BC Farming begins in the Nile Valley.
			c.3100BC King Menes unites Upper and Lower Egypt.
			c.2686BC The Old Kingdom begins in Egypt.
			c.2530BC The Egyptians start building the Great Pyramid at Giza.
		c.1900-1450BC The Minoans build palaces on Crete.	c.2040BC The Middle Kingdom begins.
			c.1720BC The Hyksos invade Egypt. The Middle Kingdom ends.
		c.1600BC The Mycenaeans become powerful in Greece.	c.1570BC The New Kingdom begins.
	c.1200BC The Olmecs build temples. The Chavín way of life begins.	c.1450BC The Mycenaeans invade Crete.	c.1450BC The Egyptian Empire is at its largest under King Tuthmosis III.
		c.1100BC The Greek Dark Ages begin.	

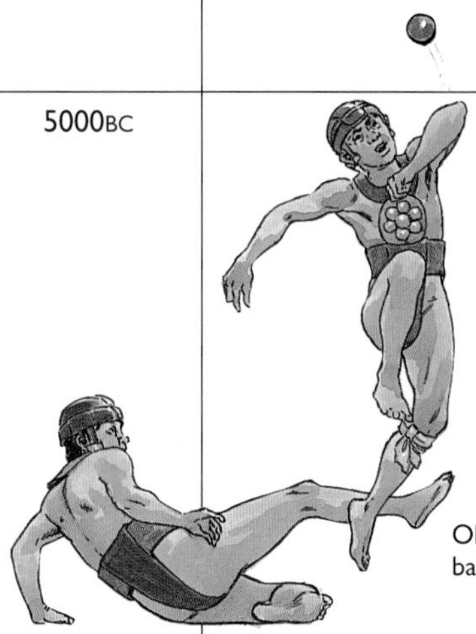

Olmec ball-players

Mycenaean woman

DATE	THE AMERICAS	EUROPE	AFRICA
1000BC	c.1000BC The Adena build earth mounds.	c.800BC The Celtic way of life spreads across western Europe.	c.814BC The city of Carthage is built by the Phoenicians.
		c.776BC The first Olympic Games.	
		753BC The city of Rome is set up, according to legend.	
		c.509BC Rome becomes a republic.	

The Great Serpent Mound

DATE	THE AMERICAS	EUROPE	AFRICA
500BC		c.500-350BC The Greeks are at their most successful.	c.500BC The Nok way of life begins.
		431-404BC The Peloponnesian War.	Nok sculpture
	c.300BC The Hopewell take over from the Adena.	356BC Alexander the Great is born.	332BC Alexander the Great conquers Egypt.
	c.200BC The Nazca start to draw lines in the desert.	44BC Julius Caesar is murdered.	146BC The Romans destroy Carthage.
		27BC Augustus becomes the first Emperor of Rome.	30BC The Romans conquer Egypt.

DATE	THE AMERICAS	EUROPE	AFRICA
AD1	c.AD1-700 The Moche are ruled by warrior-priests.	AD117 The Roman Empire is at its largest under the Emperor Trajan.	c.AD100 The kingdom of Axum becomes powerful.
	c.AD250-900 The Maya are at their most successful.	AD395 The Roman Empire splits permanently in two.	
	c.AD500 Teotihuacán is the sixth largest city in the world.	AD476 The Western Roman Empire collapses.	c.AD500 The Bantu people reach southern Africa.

A S I A			AUSTRALASIA
THE MIDDLE EAST	**SOUTH ASIA**	**THE FAR EAST**	

c.40,000BC People known as Aboriginals arrive in Australia.

Australian Aboriginal

c.10,000BC Farming begins in the Fertile Crescent.

c.9000BC The Jomon people of Japan hunt and fish for food.

c.3500BC The wheel is invented in Sumer.

Sumerian wheel

c.3500BC Farmers settle in the Indus Valley.

c.3300BC Writing is invented in Sumer.

c.2350BC Sargon of Akkad creates the world's first empire.

c.2000BC The Hittites settle in Anatolia.

c.1792-1750BC King Hammurabi rules Babylon.

c.1400BC The first alphabet is invented in Canaan.

c.1250BC The Hebrews arrive in Canaan.

c.1200BC The Phoenicians become successful sailors and traders.

c.2500-1800BC The Indus Valley people are at their most successful.

c.1500BC The Aryans arrive in the Indus Valley.

c.5000BC Farming begins in China.

c.2700BC Silk is first made.

1766-1027BC The Shang kings rule China.

c.1400BC People in China write on oracle bones.

c.1500BC People begin settling on islands in the Pacific Ocean.

c.1000-663BC The Assyrians build up a strong empire.

c.965-928BC King Solomon rules Israel.

605-562BC King Nebuchadnezzar II rules the Babylonian Empire.

559-530BC King Cyrus II rules Persia and builds up an empire.

c.560BC Siddhartha Gautama (the Buddha) is born.

1027BC The Zhou kings take control of China.

Confucius

551BC Confucius is born.

490-479BC Wars between the Persians and the Greeks.

331BC Alexander the Great defeats the Persians.

Alexander the Great

64BC The Romans conquer parts of the Middle East.

272-231BC Asoka rules the Mauryan Empire.

c.500BC Farming begins in Japan.

481-221BC The Warring States Period in China.

221BC Qin Shi Huangdi becomes China's first emperor.

202BC The Han Dynasty begins.

c.AD29 Jesus Christ is crucified.

REX IVD

Jesus on the cross

AD320-535 The Gupta Empire in India.

c.AD100 Paper is invented in China.

Yamato warrior

c.AD300 The Yamato tribe rules in Japan.

Word List

This list explains some of the more difficult words that are used in the book.

city-state A city and surrounding land, which has its own rulers.

civilization An advanced way of life, where people live in towns and have a system of laws and a way of writing.

civil war Fighting between different groups of people within the same country.

colony A settlement created in a foreign land, by people who have moved away from their homeland.

cuneiform writing An ancient form of writing made up of wedge-shaped symbols.

Clay tablet carved with cuneiform writing

democracy A system of government where the people have a say in how their country is run.

dynasty A series of rulers from the same family.

empire A large group of lands that is ruled by one powerful person or government.

fresco A picture painted on a wall while the plaster is still damp.

Fresco from the palace at Knossos on Crete

government The group of people who run a country.

hieroglyphs Picture writing.

incense A sweet-smelling substance that was burned in ancient temples or in the presence of kings.

lacquer A substance that can be painted onto wood, to make it shiny and waterproof.

Chinese bowl covered in lacquer

Middle Kingdom The second main period in Egyptian history (c.2040BC–c.1720BC).

mosaic A picture made from lots of small pieces of stone or glass.

Roman mosaic showing an actor in costume

New Kingdom The third main period in Egyptian history (c.1570BC–c.1070BC).

nomads People who have no permanent home, but who move around from place to place.

Old Kingdom The first main period in Egyptian history (c.2686BC–c.2180BC).

pharaoh An Egyptian king.

Statue of Pharaoh Tuthmosis III

province An area within an empire, such as the province of Britain in the Roman Empire.

republic A country without a king or queen, whose leaders rule on behalf of the people.

scribe A person in the ancient world whose job was to read and write for everyone else.

shrine A sacred building or place, where people worship or where something holy is kept.

state A land that has its own rulers.

ziggurat A stepped tower with a temple on top.

The ziggurat in the city of Babylon

Index

Pages where you can find out most about a subject are shown in **bold** type.

A

Abu Simbel, temple at, 32
Acropolis, 54
actors and acting, 53, 87
Adena people, 73
Adulis, port of, 69
Africa, 30, 40, 41, **68-69**, 81
Akkad, land of, **9**, 28
Alexander the Great, 35, 41, 49, **56-57**
Alexandria, city of, 57
alphabets, 36, 41
Amorites, 9, 28
amphitheatres, 86
amulets, 12
Amun, god, 32
Anatolia, 29
animals, taming of, 4, 68
Antigonas, 57
Anubis, god, 12, 32
aqueducts, 85
Arabia and Arabs, **67**, 69
archaeologists, 3
Arctic people, 73
armies, 9, 26, 29, 30, 37, 42-43, 50-51, 56, 81, 82-83, 90
Aryans, 15, **70**
Ashur,
    city of, 44, 45
    god, 44
Ashurbanipal, King, 44, 45
Ashurnasirpal II, King, 44
Asia Minor, 78, 88
Asoka, Emperor, 71
Assyria and Assyrians, 35, 39, 41, **42-45**, 46
Astarte, goddess, 36
Athene, goddess, 54
Athens, city of, 50, 51, **54-55**
Augustus, Emperor, 81, 82
Avebury stone circle, 18
Avenue of the Dead, 76
Axum, kingdom of, 69

B

Baal, god, 36
Babylon,
    city of, 28, 39, **46-47**, 57
    Hanging Gardens of, 46
Babylonians, 9, **28**, 39, 41, 45, **46-47**, 49
Bantu people, 69
barbarians, 90, 91
Basketmakers, 73
Bast, goddess, 32
baths, 14, 25, 52, 84
battering rams, 43, 83
Battle,
    of Marathon, 51
    of Plataea, 51
    of Qadesh, 29
    of Salamis, 51
beer, 7, 11
bread, 11, 24, 38
bricks, 4, 6, 34
Buddhism, 70, 71

burial of the dead, 5, 9, 12-13, 17, 19, 25, 59, 61, 63, 65, 66, 74
Byblos, city of, 36, 40
Byzantium, town of, 90

C

camels, 65, 67
Canaan and Canaanites, **36**, 37, 38, 40
canopic jars, 12
Carthage, city of, 41, 81
carts, 8, 14, 37
caste system, 70
catacombs, 89
Çatal Hüyük, town of, 5
catapults, 56, 83
Celts, 78-79
Central America, 75-77
Chandragupta Maurya, Emperor, 71
Ch'ang-an, city of, 64
chariot racing, 53, 87
chariots, 8, 9, 26, 29, 30, 42, 43, 61, 79
Chavín people, 74
China, **60-65**, 66
Chi-Ro sign, 89
Christianity, 69, **88-89**
circus, 87
cities, 6-7, 14, 15, 24, 26, 29, 36, 40, 41, 42, 43, 44, 46-47, 54, 55, 57, 64, 67, 76, 77, 90, 91
city-states, 6, 50, 54, 55, 56
Classical Period in Greece, 52
Cleopatra, Queen, 35
coffins, 12, 37
Colosseum, 86
columns, types of, 55
Confucius, 61, 64
Constantine, Emperor, 89, 90
Constantinople, city of, 90, 91
consuls, 80
cotton, 15
crafts, 4, 6, 8, 15, 19, 25, 33, 40, 58, 61, 66, 73, 74, 76, 77, 78
Crete, island of, **20-23**, 27
cuneiform writing, 7
Cyrus II, King, 48

D

dancers and dancing, 32, 34, 71
Danube, River, 16
Darius I, King, 48, 49
Dark Ages in Greece, 50
David, King, 38
democracy, 55
Dido, Princess, 41
Diocletian, Emperor, 90
Dionysus, god, 53
drama, 53, 87
druids, 79

E

Eastern Roman Empire, 90, 91
Ebla, city of, 36
Egypt and Egyptians, **10-13**, 27, 29, **30-35**, 36, 37, 38, 56, 57, 67, 68

elephants, 56, 71, 81
emperors, 62-63, 64, 66, 71, 81, 82, 86, 89, 90
Euphrates, River, 6, 7
Europa, Princess, 20
Exodus, 38
Ezana, King, 69

F

farming, 4, 6, 10-11, 14, 16, 22, 38, 44, 60, 69, 73, 74, 75, 76
feasts, 24, 79
Fertile Crescent, 4
fishing, 16, 22, 66, 73
fortresses, 14, 15
forts, 79, 83, 84
frankincense, 67, 69
frescoes, 21

G

games, 35, 75, 77, 86, 87
Germani (Germanic tribes), 90, 91
Giza, pyramids at, 13
gladiators, 86
glass, 40
gods and goddesses, 5, 6, 17, 20, 23, 28, 29, 32, 36, 44, 46, 47, 49, 53, 54, 61, 66, 70, 74, 75, 76, 77, 79, 84
Goliath, 38
Great Plains, 72
Great Pyramid, 13
Great Serpent Mound, 73
Great Stupa at Sanchi, 71
Great Wall of China, 62
Greece and Greeks, 24, 49, **50-57**, 59, 88
Gupta Empire, 71
Gutians, 9

H

Hammurabi, King, **28**, 46
Han dynasty, 64-65
Hanging Gardens of Babylon, 46
Hannibal, 81
Harappa, city of, 14
Hattushash, city of, 29
Hebrews, 37, **38-39**
Helen of Troy, 27
Hellespont, 51
Herodotus, 55
hieroglyphs, 33
hillforts, 79
Hinduism, 70
Hittites, 28, **29**, 30, 36, 37
Hopewell people, 73
hoplites, 50, 51
Horus, god, 32
houses, 4, 5, 6, 7, 14, 16-17, 22, 34, 38, 52, 60, 64, 66, 69, 73, 76, 78, 84, 85
Huns, 62, 65, 91
hunting,
    for food, 4, 16, 59, 66, 68, 69, 72, 73
    for fun, 26, 35, 45
Hyksos people, 30

I

igloos, 73
incense, 30, 32, 45, 48, **67**
India, 56, 57, 67, 68, 69, **70-71**
Indus Valley people, 14-15
Ishtar,
    Gate, 46
    goddess, 46, 47
Isis, goddess, 32
Israel, kingdom of, 38, 39

J

Japan, 66
Jericho, town of, 5
Jerusalem, city of, 38, 39, 47, 88
Jesus Christ, 88
Jews, 39, 88
Jomon Period in Japan, 66
Judah, kingdom of, 39, 47
Judea, province of, 88
Julius Caesar, 81
Jupiter, god, 84

K

Kassites, 46
Khafre, pyramid of, 13
Khufu, pyramid of, 13
Knossos, palace at, **20-21**, 27
K'ung Fu-tzu (Confucius), 61
Kush, kingdom of, 68

L

lacquer, 64, 65
laws, 28, 39, 55, 63, 64, 80, 84
legend,
    of King Minos, 20
    of the Minotaur, 21
    of Romulus and Remus, 80
    of the Trojan horse, 27
legionaries, Roman, 82, 83
Lepenski Vir, village of, 16
libraries, 33, 45
lighthouse at Alexandria, 57
Linear A writing, 22
Linear B writing, 25
Lion Gate,
    at Hattushash, 29
    at Mycenae, 26
Liu Bang, Emperor, 64
llamas, 74
Lothal, port of, 15
Lower Egypt, 10

M

Ma'at, goddess, 32
Macedonia, kingdom of, 56, 57
Magi, 49
mammoths, 72
Marathon, Battle of, 51
Marduk, god, 28, 46, 47
Ma'rib, city of, 67
Mark Antony, 81
markets, 8, 15, 22, 54, 64, 85
mastaba tombs, 13
Mauryan Empire, 71
Maximian, Emperor, 90

Maya people, 77
Medes, 45, 46, **48**, 49
Media, kingdom of, 45, 46, **48**
Memphis, city of, 10
Menes, King, 10
merchants, 8, 22, 27, 30, 36, 40, 41, 59, 65, 67, 69, 76
Meroë, city of, 68
Mesopotamia, 6
metalwork, 8, 19, 61, 66, 68, 78
Middle Kingdom of Egypt, 12, 13
Minoans, **20-23**, 27
Minos, King, 20, 21
Minotaur, 21
Mitannian Empire, 29
Mithridates, King, 59
Moche people, 74
Mohenjo-daro, city of, 14, 15
monks, Buddhist, 71
mosaics, 75, 85
Moses, 38
mummies, 12
murex (shellfish), 40
music and musicians, 23, 24, 32, 34, 44, 52, 71
Mycenae, city of, 24, 25, 26
Mycenaeans, 23, **24-27**, 50
myrrh, 30, 67, 69

N
Nabataea, kingdom of, 67
Nabopolassar, King, 46
Nanna, god, 6
Napata, city of, 68
natron, 12
Nazca people, 74
Nebuchadnezzar II, King, 46, 47
New Kingdom of Egypt, 12, 13
Next World, 12, 19, 59, 61, 65
Nile, River, 10, 31, 32
Nimrud, city of, 44
Nineveh, city of, 44, 45
nobles, 9, 26, 34, 35, 61, 62, 64
Nok people, 68
nomads, 38, 58, 67
North America, 72-73
Nubia and Nubians, 30, 31, 35
numbers, 77

O
obelisks, 33
Octavian, 81
Odoacer, King, 91
officials, 7, 48, 49, 54, 64
Ohio River, 73
Old Kingdom of Egypt, 12, 13
Olmecs, 75
Olympic Games, 53
oracle bones, 61
Osiris, god, 32

P
palaces, 20-21, 24, 25, 44, 46, 49
paper, invention of, 65
papyrus, 3, 33
Paracas people, 74
Parthenon, 54, 55

parties, 34, 52
pastimes, 35, 53, 86-87
Paul of Tarsus, 88
Peleset tribe, 37
Peloponnesian War, 55
Perikles, 54
Persepolis, palace of, **49**, 56
Persia and Persians, 35, 41, 47, **48-49**, 51, 54, 56
Persian Wars, 49, **51**, 54
Peru, 74
Petra, city of, 67
pharaohs, 13, 30, 31, 35
Pharos lighthouse, 57
Philip II, King, 56
Philistines, 37, 38
Phoenicia and Phoenicians, 39, **40-41**
pictograms (picture writing), 7, 22
pillars, types of, 55
Plataea, Battle of, 51
Plato, 55
poets and poetry, 24, 26, 71, 79
Pompeii, town of, 85
Porus, King, 56
pots and pottery, 4, 8, 15, 22, 25, 33, 54, 60, 66, 74, 76
priests and priestesses, 5, 12, 13, 14, 23, 25, 32, 36, 39, 47, 49, 61, 67, 70, 74, 79
Ptolemy family, 35, 57
Punic Wars, 81
Punt, land of, 30
Pyramid of the Moon, 76
Pyramid of the Sun, 76
pyramids, 13, 68, 76
Pythagoras, 55

Q
Qadesh, Battle of, 29
quetzal bird, 76
Qin, kingdom of, 62
Qin Shi Huangdi, Emperor, 62-63

R
Ramesses II, King, 30
Ramesses III, King, 35
Re, god, 32
religion, 5, 6, 8, 12, 13, 14, 17, 18, 23, 28, 29, 32, 36, 38, 39, 44, 46, 47, 49, 53, 54, 61, 67, 70, 71, 74, 75, 76, 77, 79, 84, 88-89
roads, 48, 63, 64, 65, 83
Roman Empire, 79, 82, 83, 84, 88, 89, 90-91
Roman Republic, 80
Romans, 35, 41, 57, 69, 79, **80-87**, 88, **89**, **90-91**
Rome, city of, 80, 86, 88, 89, 91
Romulus and Remus, 80
round barrows, 19

S
Sabaea, kingdom of, 67
sacrifices,
    animal, 9, 17, 23, 25, 32, 36, 59, 61, 79

human, 9, 59, 61, 74, 75, 77, 79
Sahara Desert, 68
Salamis, Battle of, 51
Sardis, city of, 48
Sargon of Akkad, King, 9
satraps, 48
Saul, King, 38
Scandinavia, 19
schools, 33, 52, 84
science, 55, 65
scribes, 8, 25, 31, 33, 36, 43, 44
Scythians, 49, **58-59**
seals (for stamping words), 15
Sea Peoples, 29, 35, 36, **37**
Seleucid Empire, 57
Senate and senators, 80, 81
shaduf, 10, 44
Shang dynasty, 61
Sheba, Queen of, 67
Sherden tribe, 37
ships, 8, 15, 22, 27, 31, 36, 37, 40, 41, 50, 51
Shiva, god, 70
shrines, 5, 23, 32, 34, 36, 46
Shuppiluliuma, King, 29
Siddhartha Gautama (the Buddha), 70
Sidon, city of, 40
silk, 60
Silk Road, 65
Sinai, 30, 31
Skara Brae, 17
skulls, 5, 58, 78
slaves, 9, 28, 36, 39, 47, 52, 54, 55, 58, 69, 83, 85, 86
Socrates, 55
soldiers, 9, 26, 37, 42-43, 48, 50-51, 55, 56, 81, 82-83, 84, 90
Solomon, King, **39**, 67
South America, 74
Sparta, city of, **50**, 55
Sphinx, 13
spinning, 38, 52
sport, 23, 35, 53, 75, 86, 87
Stonehenge, 18-19
stupas, 71
Sumer and Sumerians, **6-9**, 15, 28
Susa, city of, 48
Sweet Track, 17
Syria and Syrians, 8, 29, 31

T
Tarxien, temples at, 17
Taweret, goddess, 32
taxes, 31, 42, 48, 64, 84
temples, 6, 7, 13, 17, 32-33, 39, 54, 55, 74, 75, 76, 77, 84
Ten Commandments, 39
tents, 38, 58, 67, 72, 83
Teotihuacán, city of, 76
terracotta warriors, 63
Teshub, god, 29
Theodosius, Emperor, 89
Thera, island of, 23
Theseus, Prince, 21
Thoth, god, 32
Tiber, River, 80

Tigris, River, 6, 42
togas, 80
toilets, 14, 84
tombs, 9, 12, 13, 17, 19, 25, 59, 61, 63, 65, 66, 67, 68, 69
towns, 5, 22, 84-85
toys, 15, 35, 87
trade, 8, 15, 19, 22, 27, 30, 31, 36, 40, 59, 65, 67, 69, 73, 76
Trajan, Emperor, 82
travel and transport, 8, 14, 22, 26, 27, 29, 30, 31, 36, 37, 40, 41, 42, 48, 64, 65
treasure, 9, 12, 19, 25, 59, 61, 65
tribute, 31
triremes, 51
Troy, siege of, 27
Tutankhamun, King, 12, 13
Tuthmosis III, King, 30
Tyre, city of, 40, 56

U
Ugarit, city of, 36
Upper Egypt, 10
Ur, city of, 6-7, 9

V
Valley of the Kings, 13
Vandals, 91
Vedas, 70
villages, 4, 16-17, 60, 66, 73, 80
Visigoths, 91
volcanoes, 23, 85

W
wall paintings, 21, 31, 33, 71, 85
war, 9, 26, 27, 29, 30, 37, 38, 42-43, 50-51, 56, 58, 61, 62, 71, 77, 79, 81, 82-83, 90, 91
warriors, 26, 29, 37, 38, 50, 58, 66, 74, 77, 79, 90, 91
weapons, 19, 26, 29, 37, 42, 43, 50, 58, 78, 79, 82, 83, 90
weaving, 4, 33, 52, 74, 78
Western Roman Empire, 90, 91
wheel, invention of, 8
wine, 11
wooden horse of Troy, 27
wood henges, 18
writing, 3, 7, 15, 22, 25, 33, 36, 41, 61, 63, 66, 77

X
Xerxes I, King, 49
Xianyang, city of, 62

Y
Yamato tribe, 66
Yangtze River, 60
Yellow River, 60

Z
Zarathustra (Zoroaster), 49
Zeus, god, 20, 53, 57
Zhou dynasty, 61
ziggurats, 6, 46

Picture credits: AKG London/Jean-Louis Nou, 67; e.t.archive, 21; Robert Harding Picture Library/Robert Frerck, 77/James Green, 55/J.E Stevenson, 85; N.J. Saunders, 75; Nicholas Shea, 18; The Stock Market, 32; Tony Stone Images/Julian Calder, 63.

First published in 1999 by Usborne Publishing Ltd, Usborne House, 83-85 Saffron Hill, London EC1N 8RT, England. www.usborne.com Copyright © 1999 Usborne Publishing Ltd.

First published in America 1999 UE. The name Usborne and the device ⚽ are Trade Marks of Usborne Publishing Ltd. All rights reserved. No part of this publication may be reproduced, stored in a retrieval system, or transmitted in any form or by any means, electronic, mechanical, photocopying, recording or otherwise, without the prior permission of the publisher. Printed in Dubai.